awakenAdream
dreamAwake
a
m
a
m

This book is
dedicated to
all the sistars
si(yes) stars(radiant)
sistars(yes, radiant females).
Similar to the moon,
from the darkness we rise.
It is our light and love
that connects us ALL.
Together we stand,
moving beyond comparison,
relinquishing competition,
reclaiming feminine power,
befriending ourselves,
speaking for the silenced,
honoring the highest integrity,
spreading loving kindness,
sharing respect,
taking up space,
and shifting energy
for the love of all.

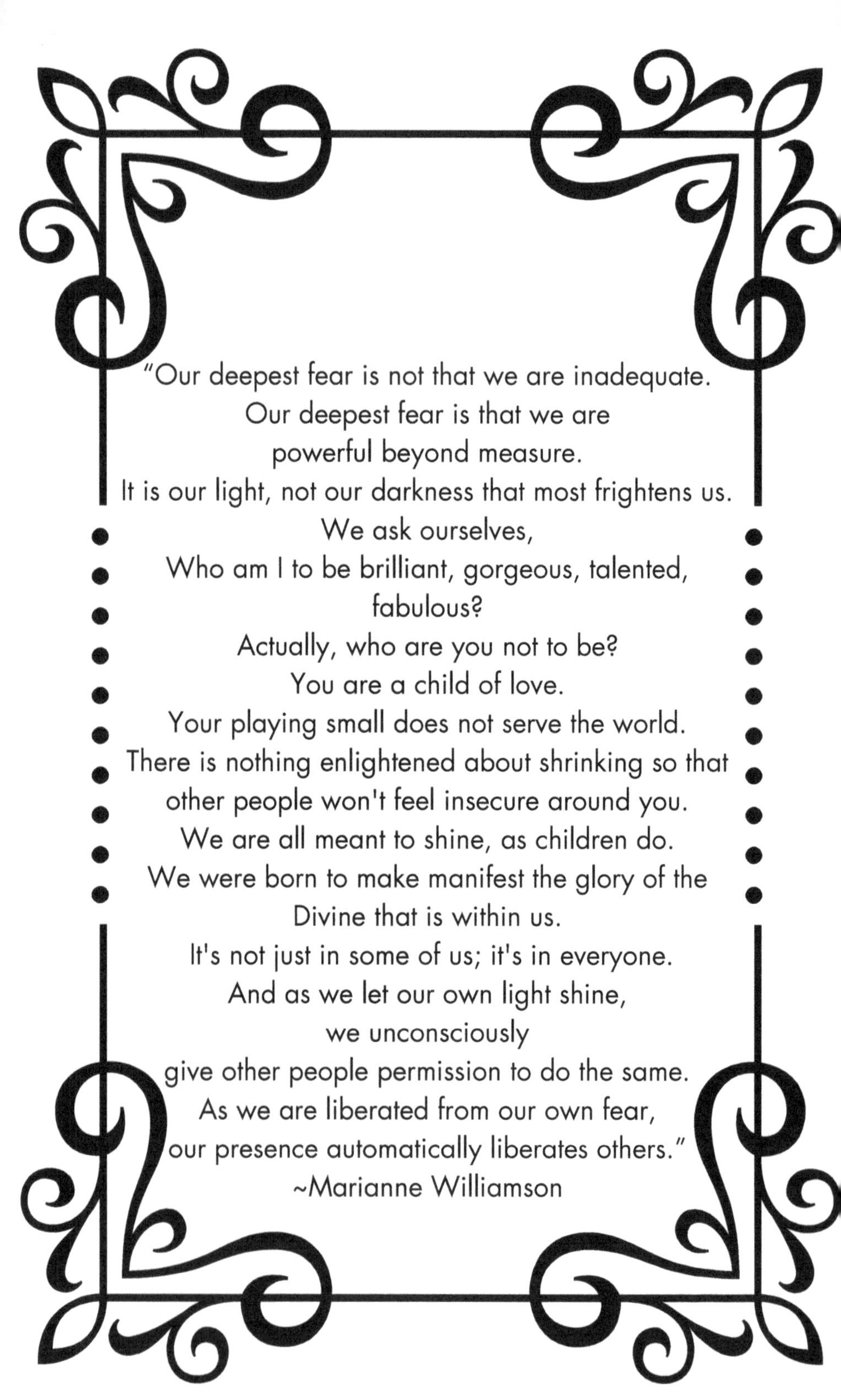

"Our deepest fear is not that we are inadequate.
Our deepest fear is that we are
powerful beyond measure.
It is our light, not our darkness that most frightens us.
We ask ourselves,
Who am I to be brilliant, gorgeous, talented,
fabulous?
Actually, who are you not to be?
You are a child of love.
Your playing small does not serve the world.
There is nothing enlightened about shrinking so that
other people won't feel insecure around you.
We are all meant to shine, as children do.
We were born to make manifest the glory of the
Divine that is within us.
It's not just in some of us; it's in everyone.
And as we let our own light shine,
we unconsciously
give other people permission to do the same.
As we are liberated from our own fear,
our presence automatically liberates others."
~Marianne Williamson

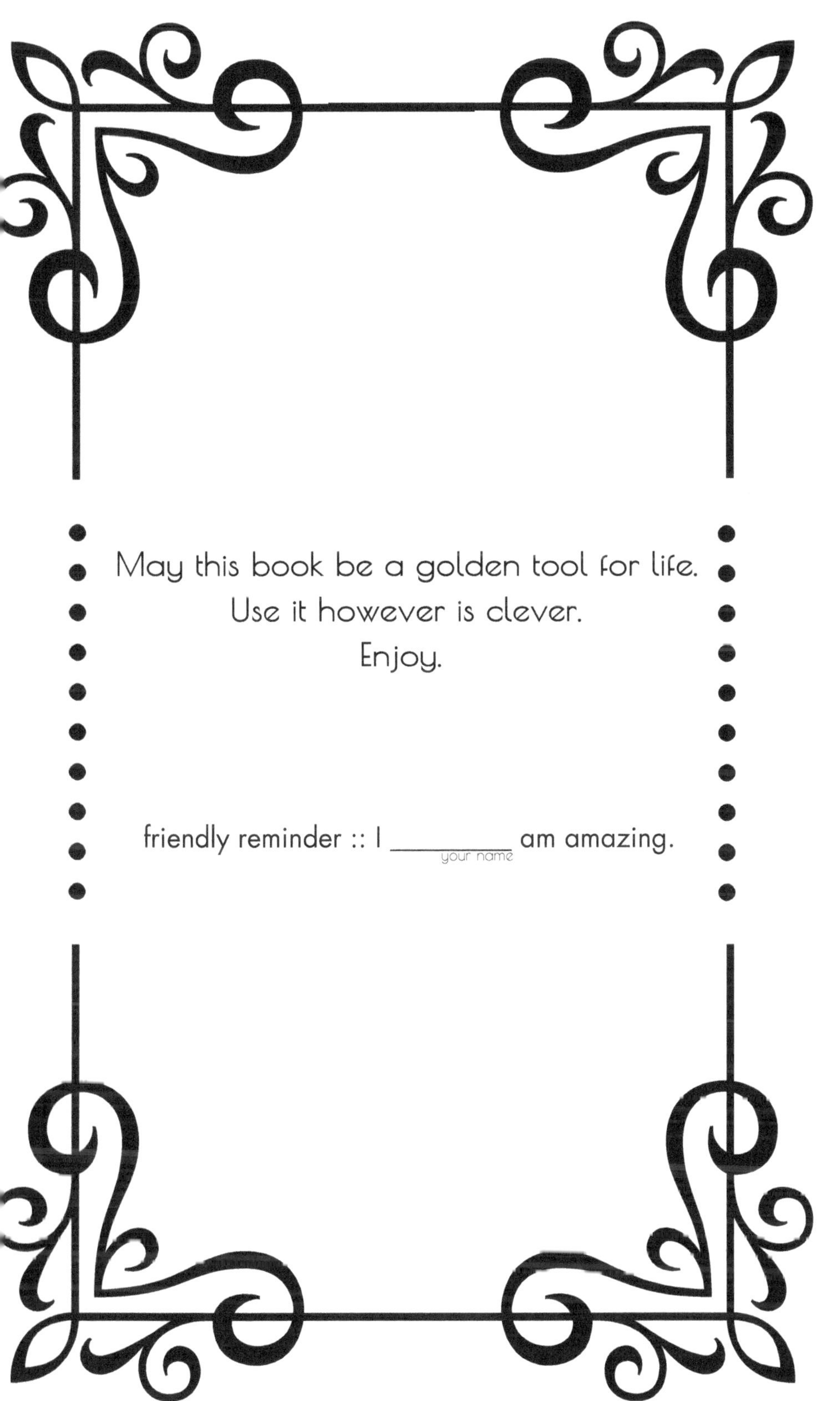
May this book be a golden tool for life.
Use it however is clever.
Enjoy.

friendly reminder :: I __________ am amazing.
your name

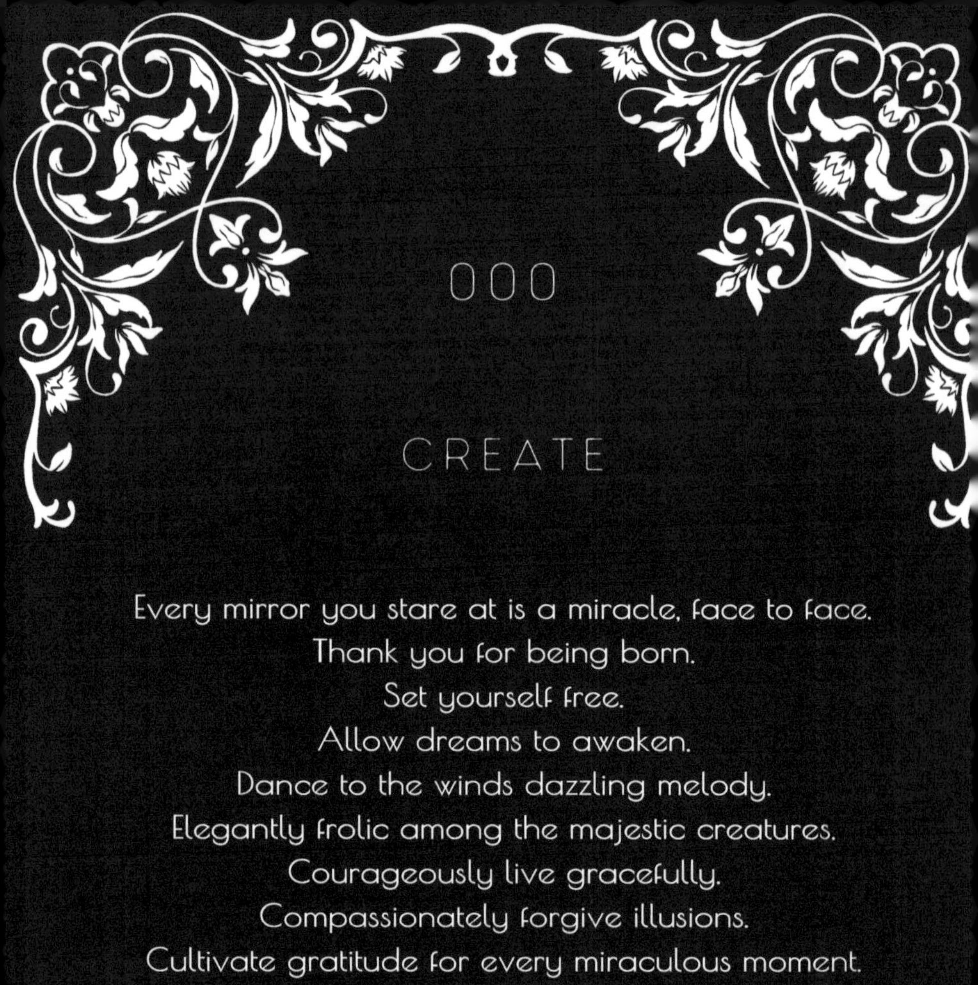

000

CREATE

Every mirror you stare at is a miracle, face to face.
Thank you for being born.
Set yourself free.
Allow dreams to awaken.
Dance to the winds dazzling melody.
Elegantly frolic among the majestic creatures.
Courageously live gracefully.
Compassionately forgive illusions.
Cultivate gratitude for every miraculous moment.
Love eternally.
May the joy for life give you freedom to be you
and the power to shine on!

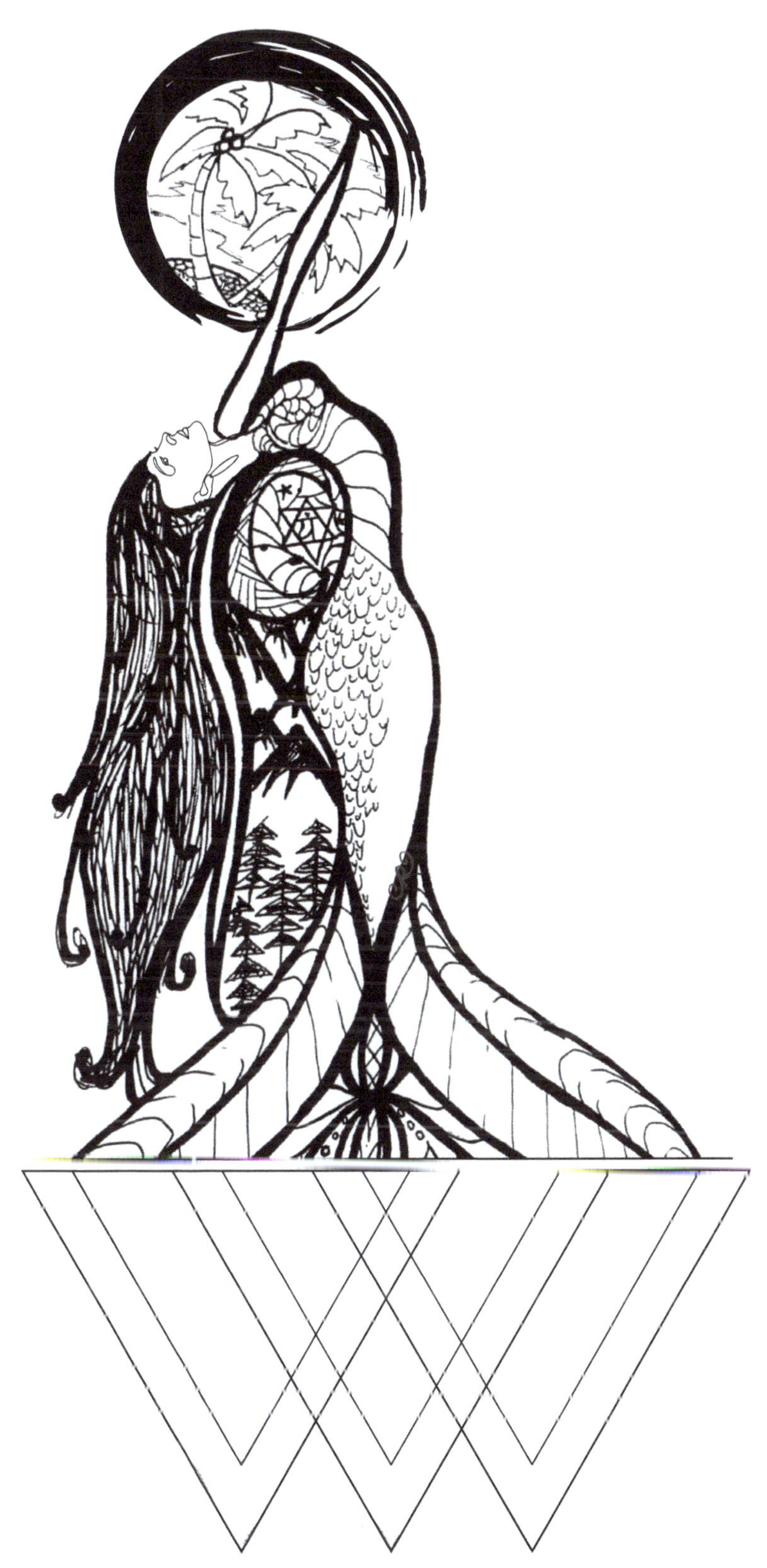

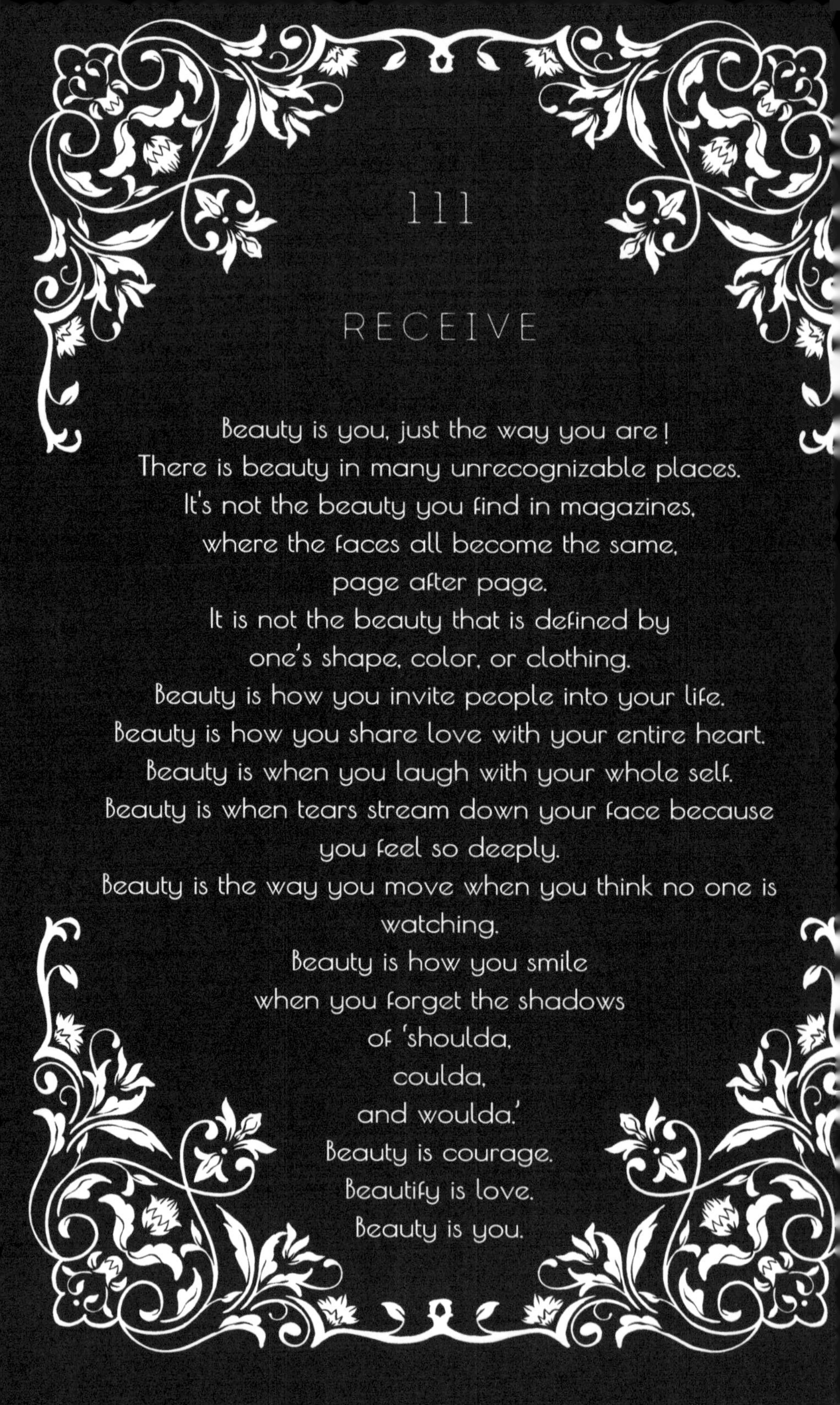

111

RECEIVE

Beauty is you, just the way you are!
There is beauty in many unrecognizable places.
It's not the beauty you find in magazines,
where the faces all become the same,
page after page.
It is not the beauty that is defined by
one's shape, color, or clothing.
Beauty is how you invite people into your life.
Beauty is how you share love with your entire heart.
Beauty is when you laugh with your whole self.
Beauty is when tears stream down your face because
you feel so deeply.
Beauty is the way you move when you think no one is
watching.
Beauty is how you smile
when you forget the shadows
of 'shoulda,
coulda,
and woulda.'
Beauty is courage.
Beautify is love.
Beauty is you.

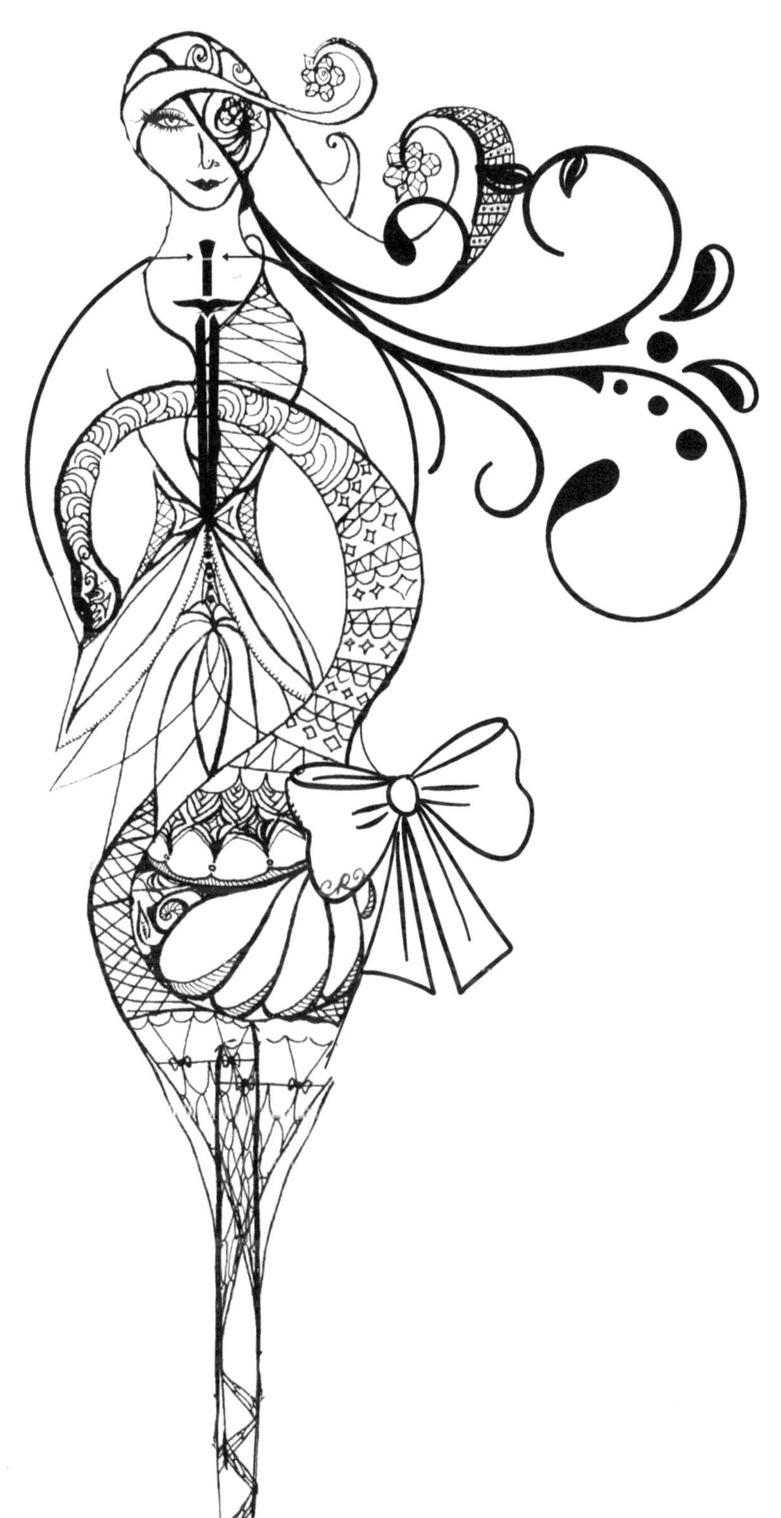

CONTEMPLATION

Look within.
Galaxies exist.
Illumination thrives.
Every win comes from within.
Energy flows where attention goes.
Every single thing we focus on manifests.
Be mindful.
Be aware.
You are a visionary, creator, manifestor!
Fall in love with what you are passionate about.
dreamAwake.
awakenAdream.
May all your wildest dreams come true.

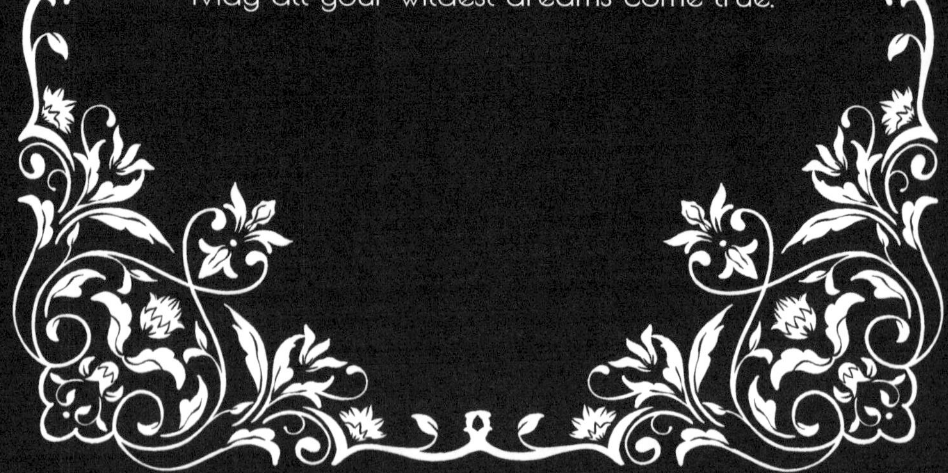

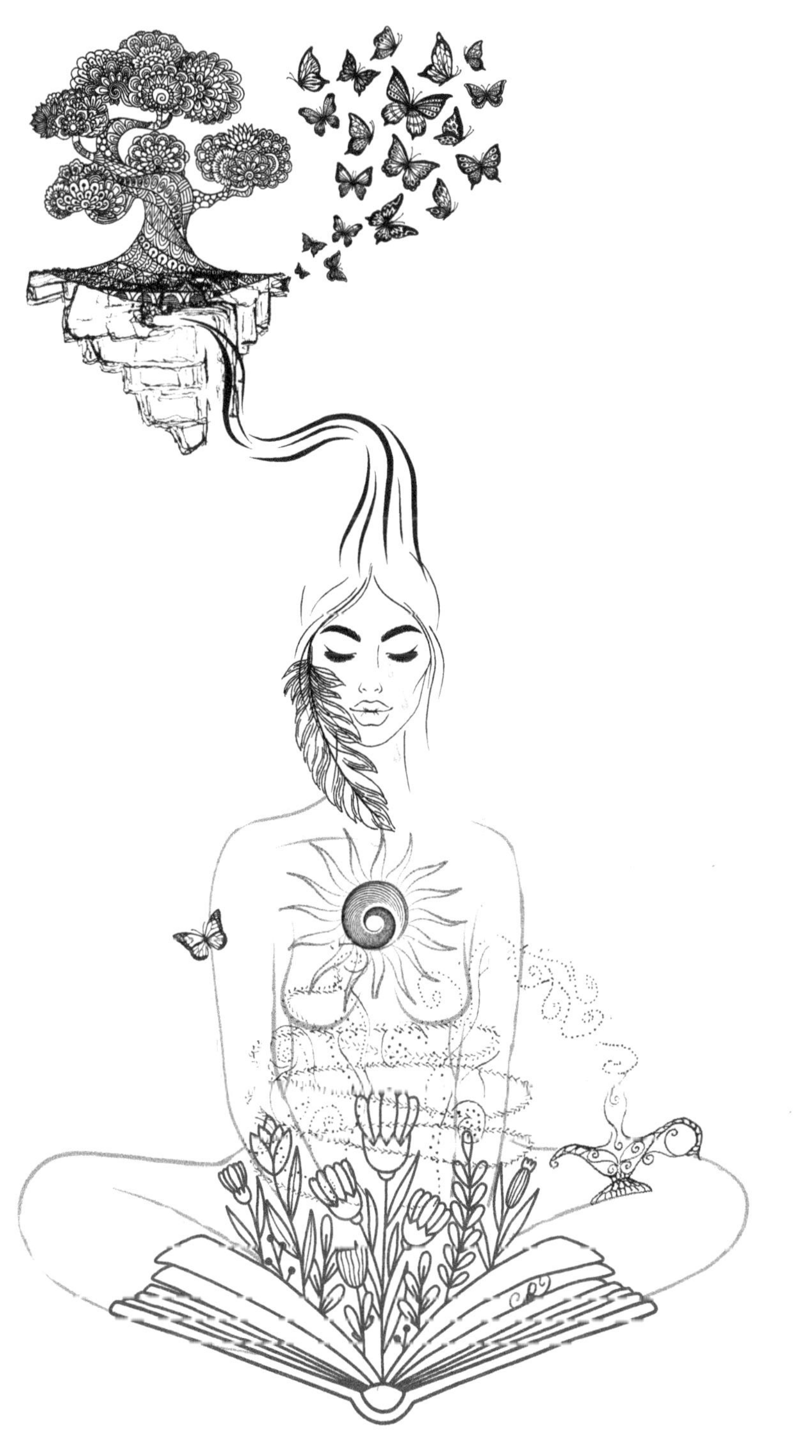

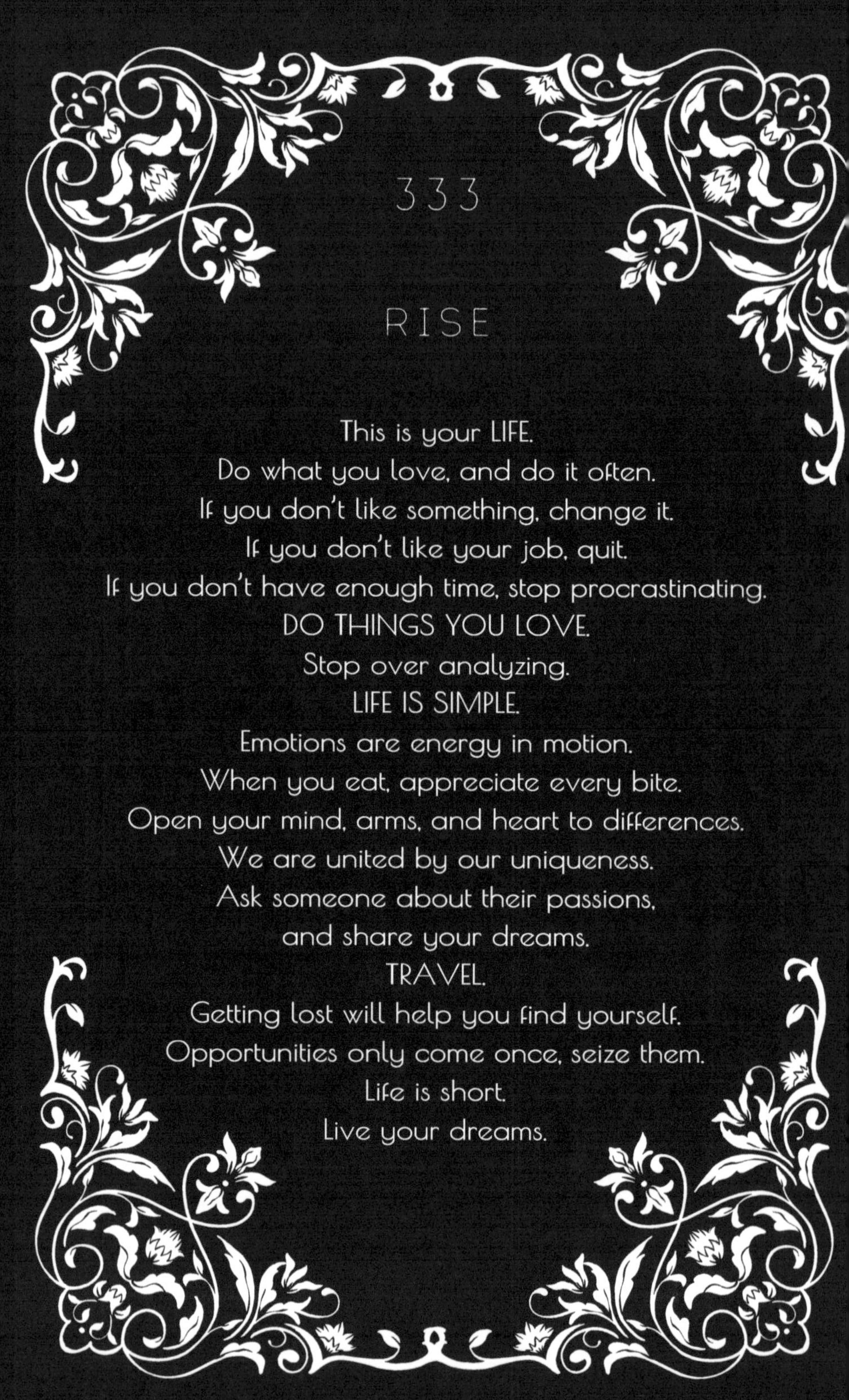

333

RISE

This is your LIFE.
Do what you love, and do it often.
If you don't like something, change it.
If you don't like your job, quit.
If you don't have enough time, stop procrastinating.
DO THINGS YOU LOVE.
Stop over analyzing.
LIFE IS SIMPLE.
Emotions are energy in motion.
When you eat, appreciate every bite.
Open your mind, arms, and heart to differences.
We are united by our uniqueness.
Ask someone about their passions,
and share your dreams.
TRAVEL.
Getting lost will help you find yourself.
Opportunities only come once, seize them.
Life is short.
Live your dreams.

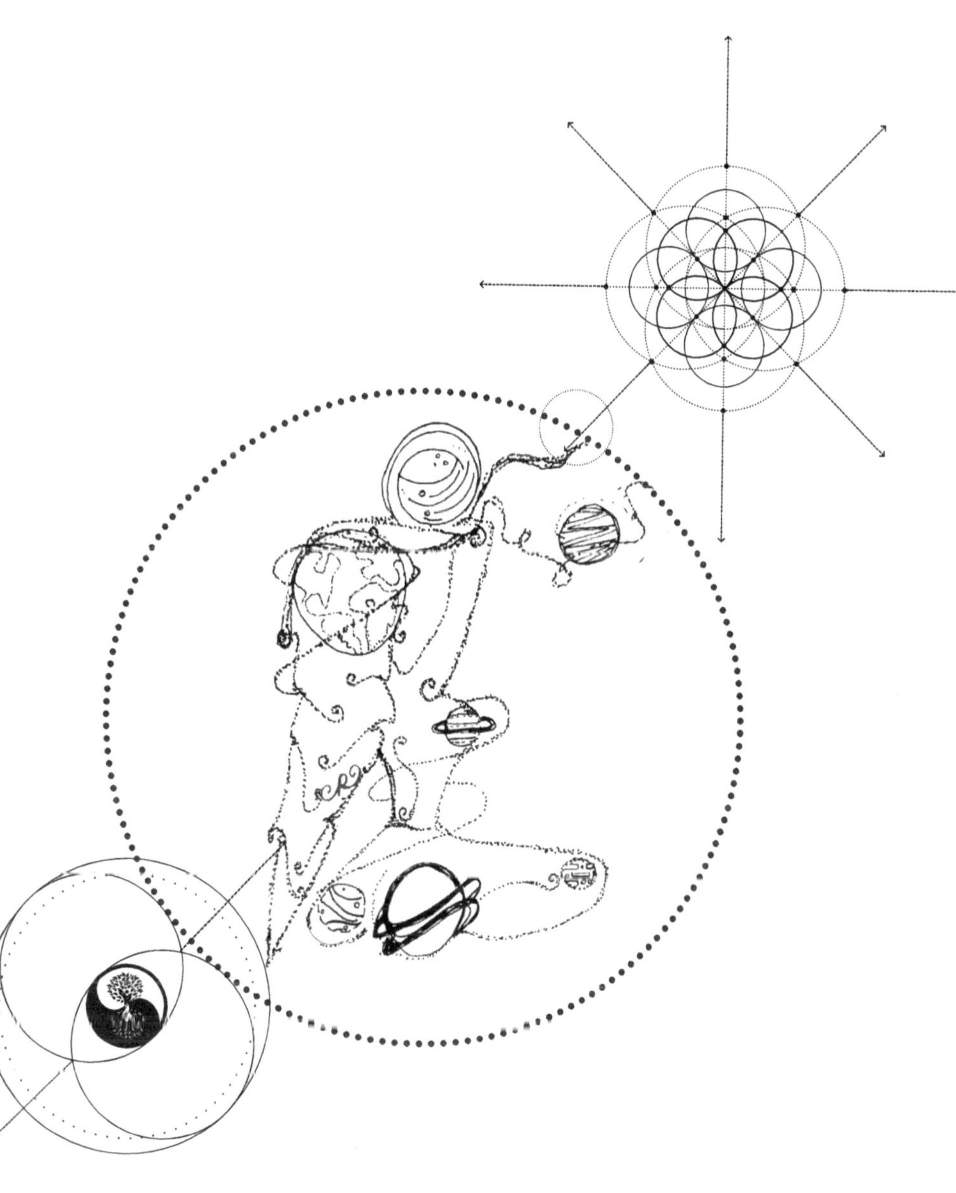

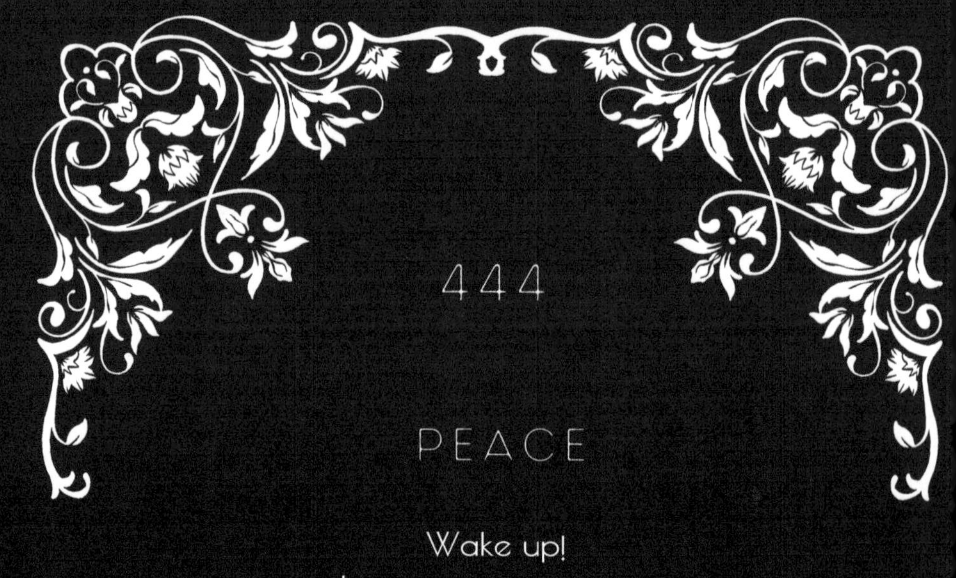

444

PEACE

Wake up!
Lessen your suffering.
Put down the stick and pick up a magical wand.
Why seek happiness outside yourself?
Happiness is within.
Why search for a truth in words?
The truth is within.
Why trust the beliefs of others?
Believe in yourself.
Why fear love?
Love is all there is.
Happiness, truth, and love
is the innate power that thrives within you.
Use the power!
Shine on Beautiful being!
SHINE ON!!!

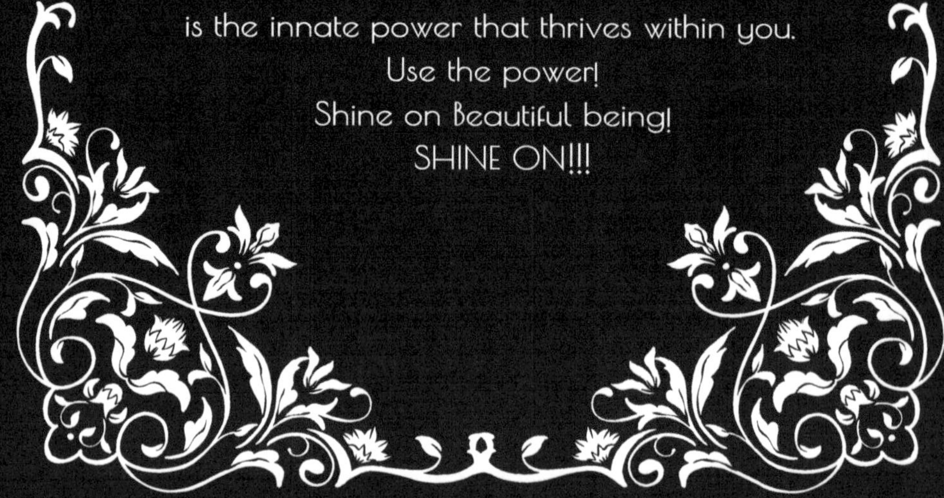

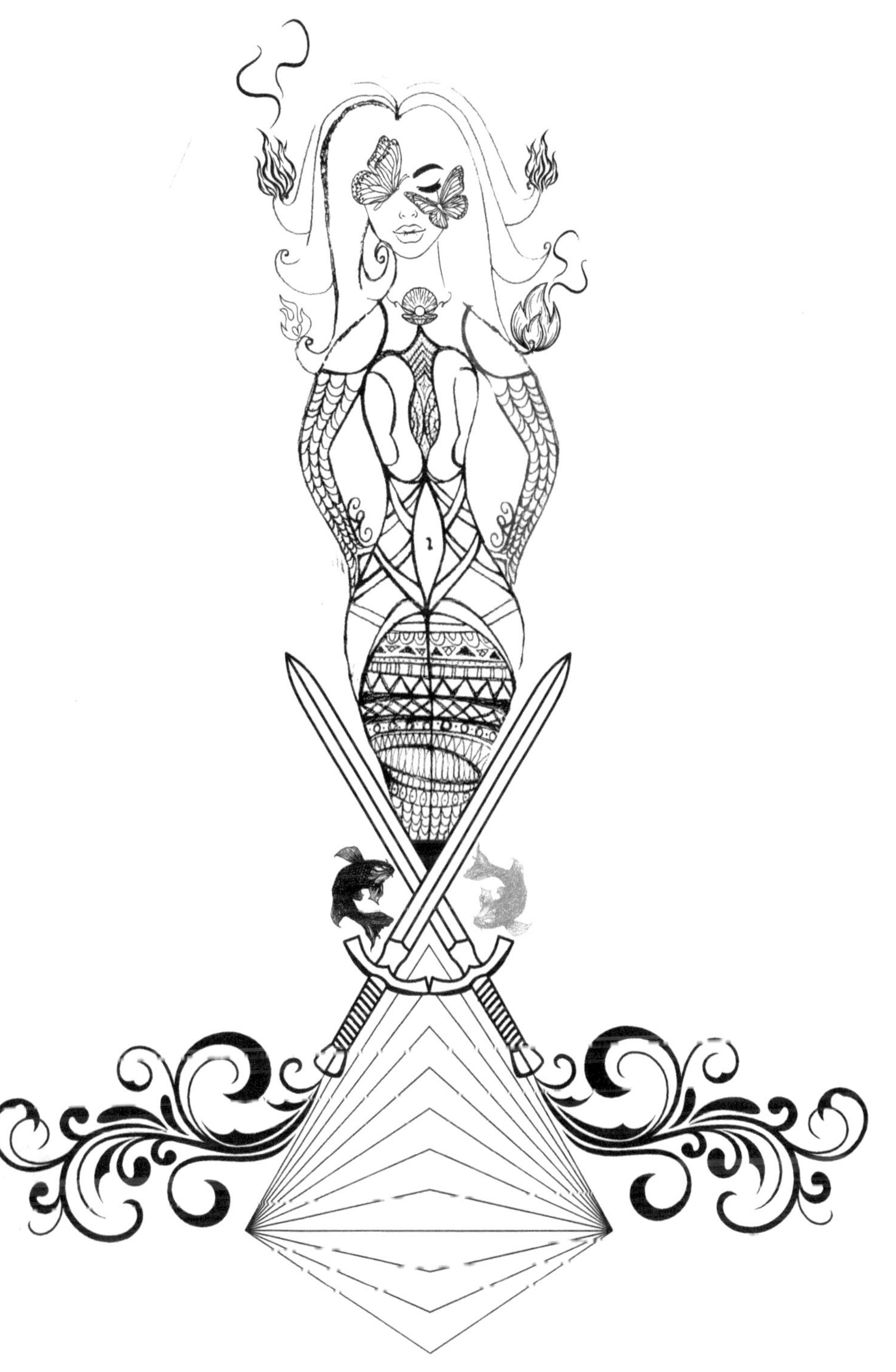

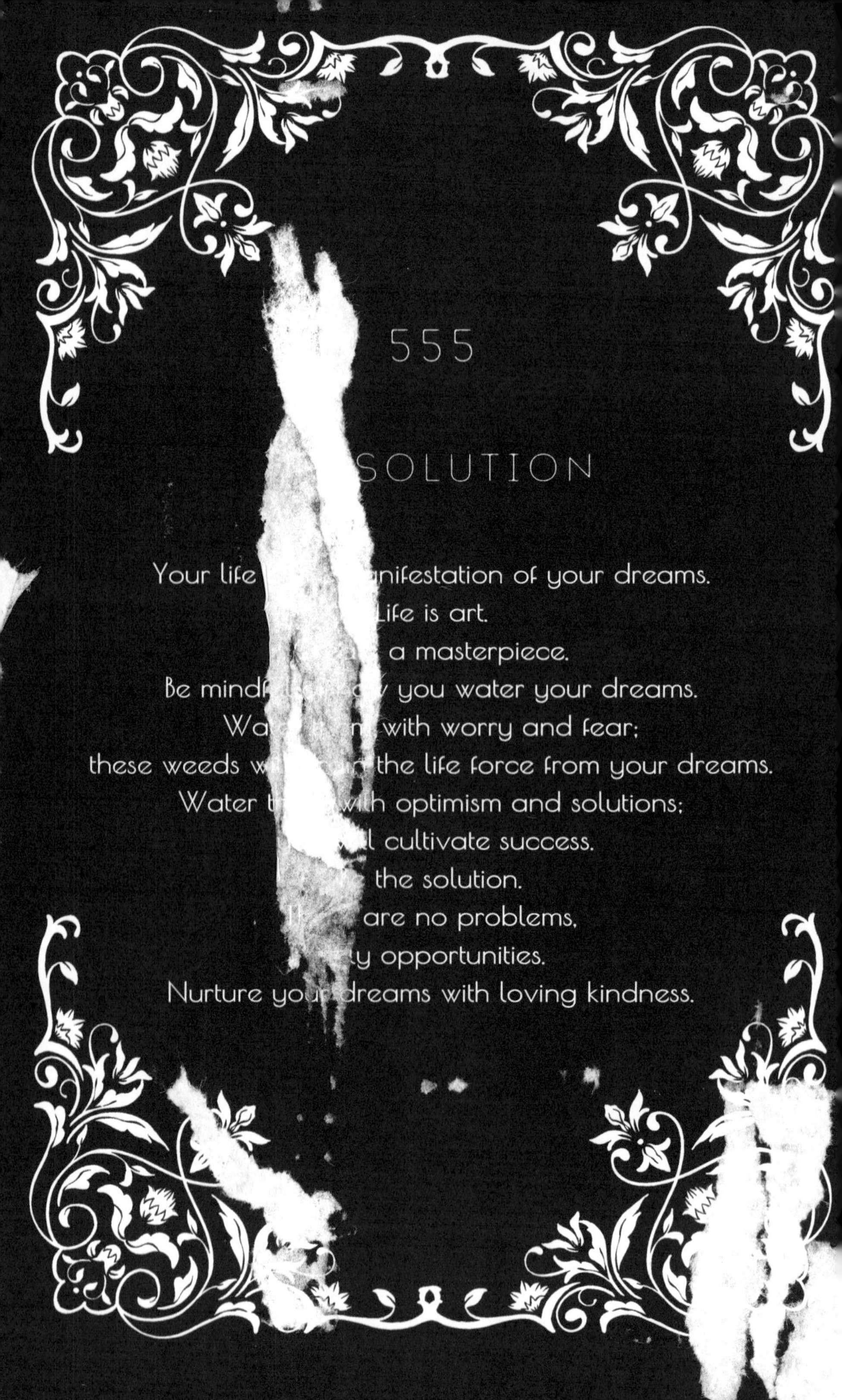

555

SOLUTION

Your life is the manifestation of your dreams.
Life is art.
a masterpiece.
Be mindful of how you water your dreams.
Water them with worry and fear;
these weeds will drain the life force from your dreams.
Water them with optimism and solutions;
will cultivate success.
the solution.
are no problems,
opportunities.
Nurture your dreams with loving kindness.

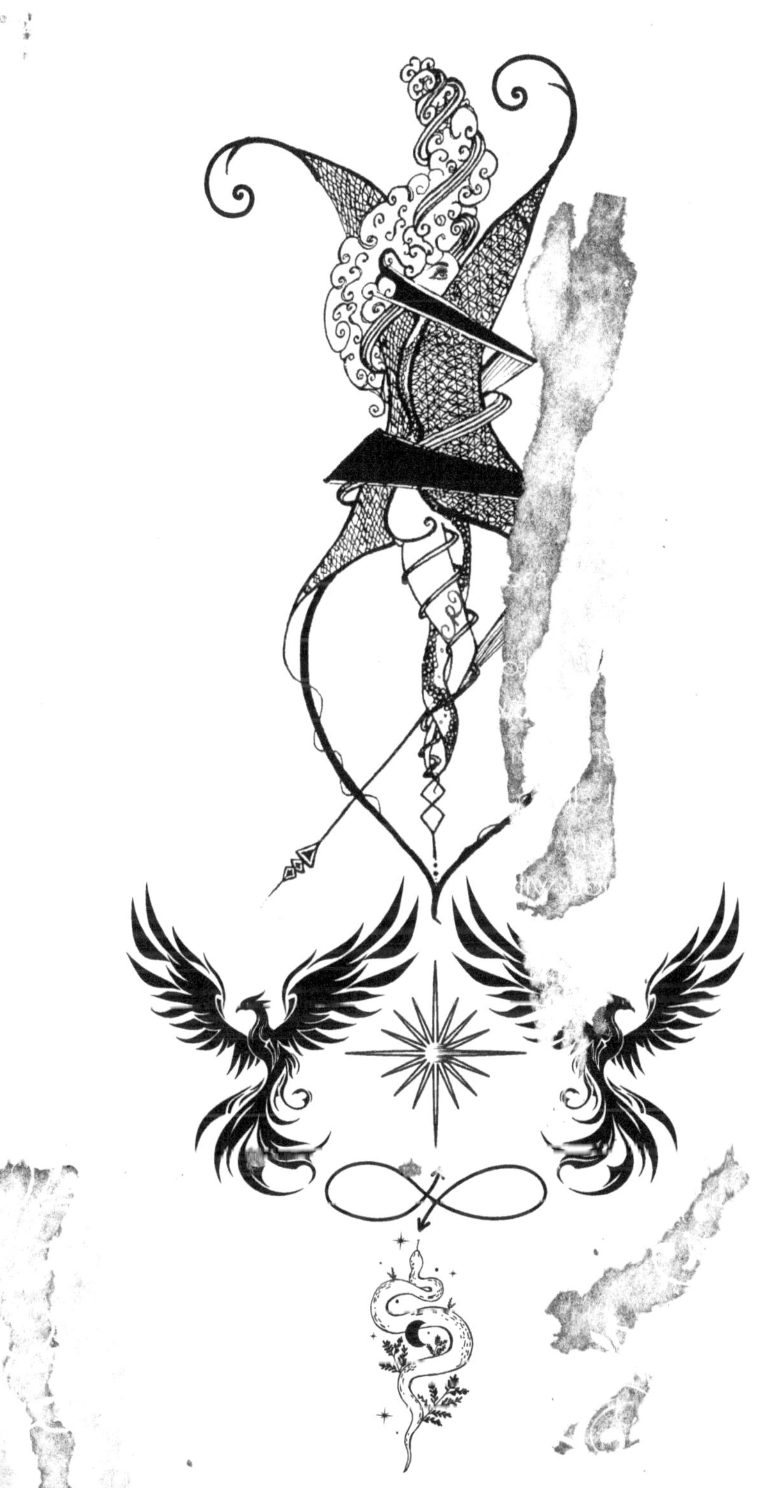

666

RETREAT

Doing is the purpose of the body.
Being is the purpose of the soul.
Let go of comforts.
Free yourself from habits.
Be the change.
Spread your magical, florescent wings.
Harness self-awareness.
Be self-observant.
Gracefully transform.

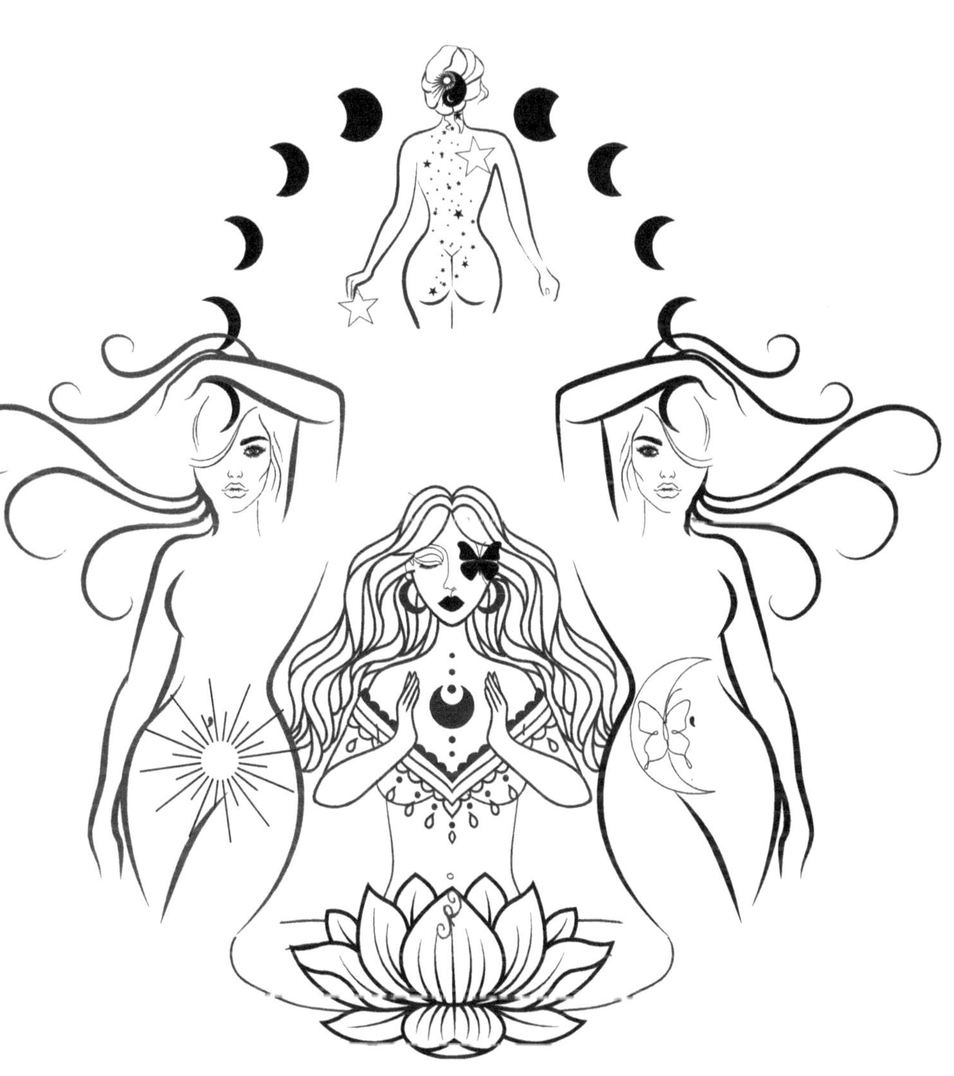

777

POWER

Life isn't about waiting for the storm to pass,
it is about learning to dance in the rain.
Be powerful.
Be all that you are.
Reclaim your power.
Honor your power.
Your beauty inspires growth in others.
To be beautiful means to be yourself.
Accept yourself.
Thank you for being you.

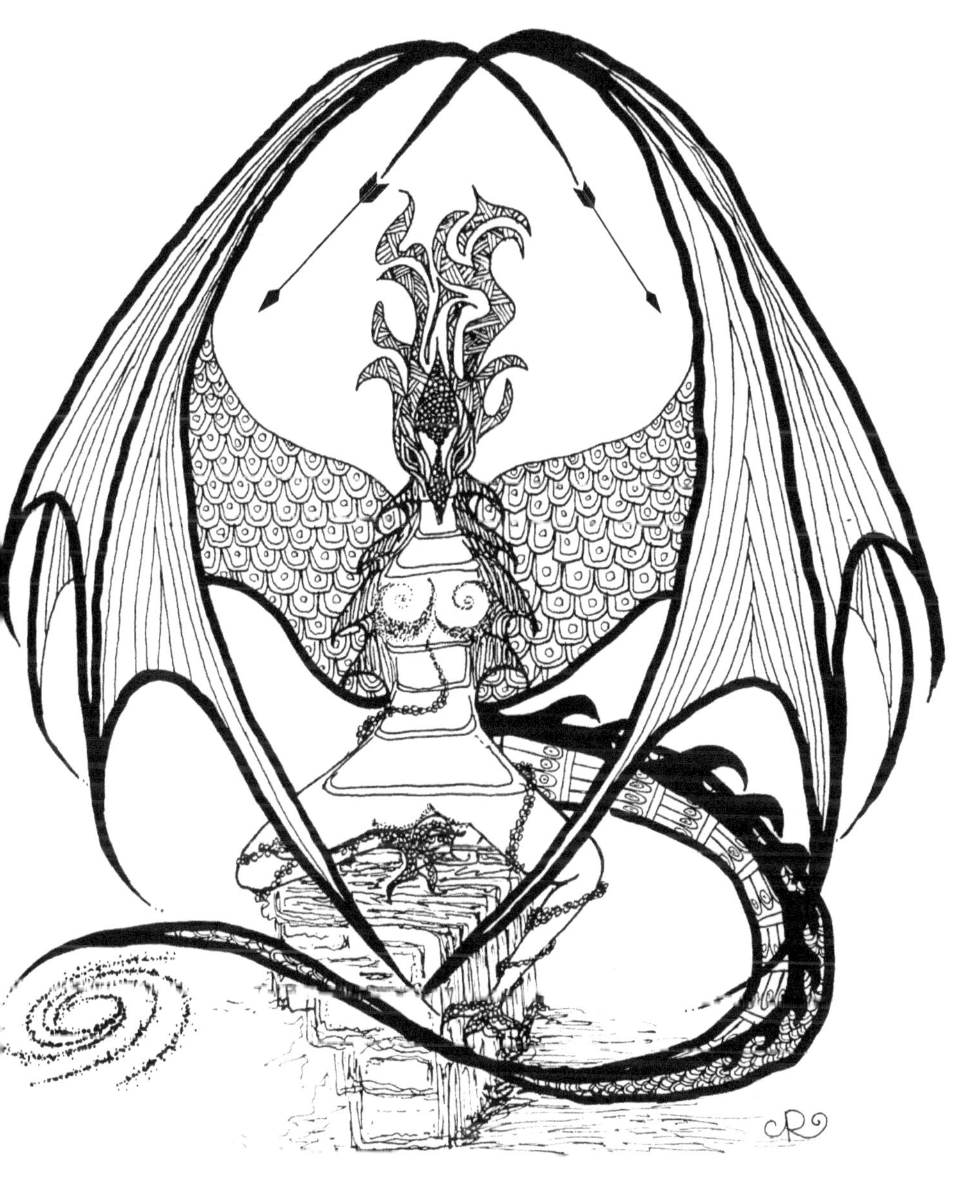

888

ENCOUNTERING

Love to live.
A smile brings light to the darkest corners.
Laughter creates joy in all.
Peace brings tranquility
when fear lingers in the shadows.
Live to love.
Honor the light within all beings.
Share compassion with grace and tenderness.
Courageously open your heart to love
again and again.
Expand your elegant wings
to reach profound potentiality.
Fly strong and free.

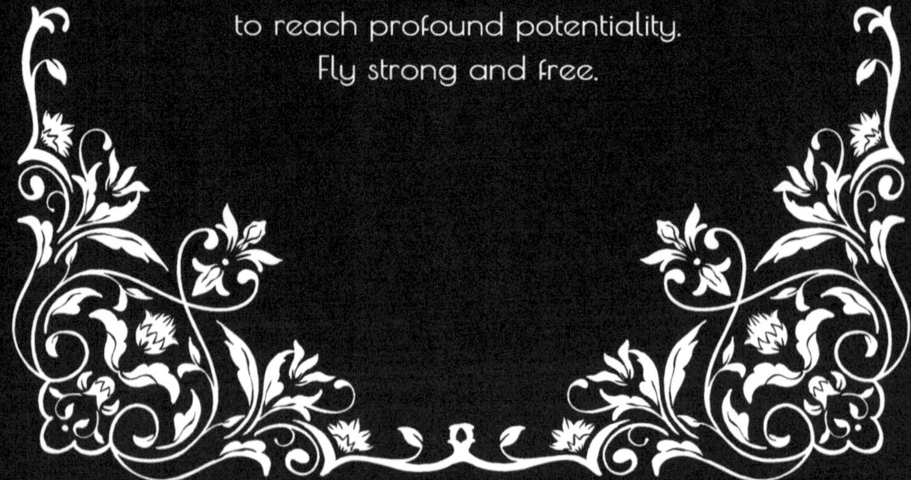

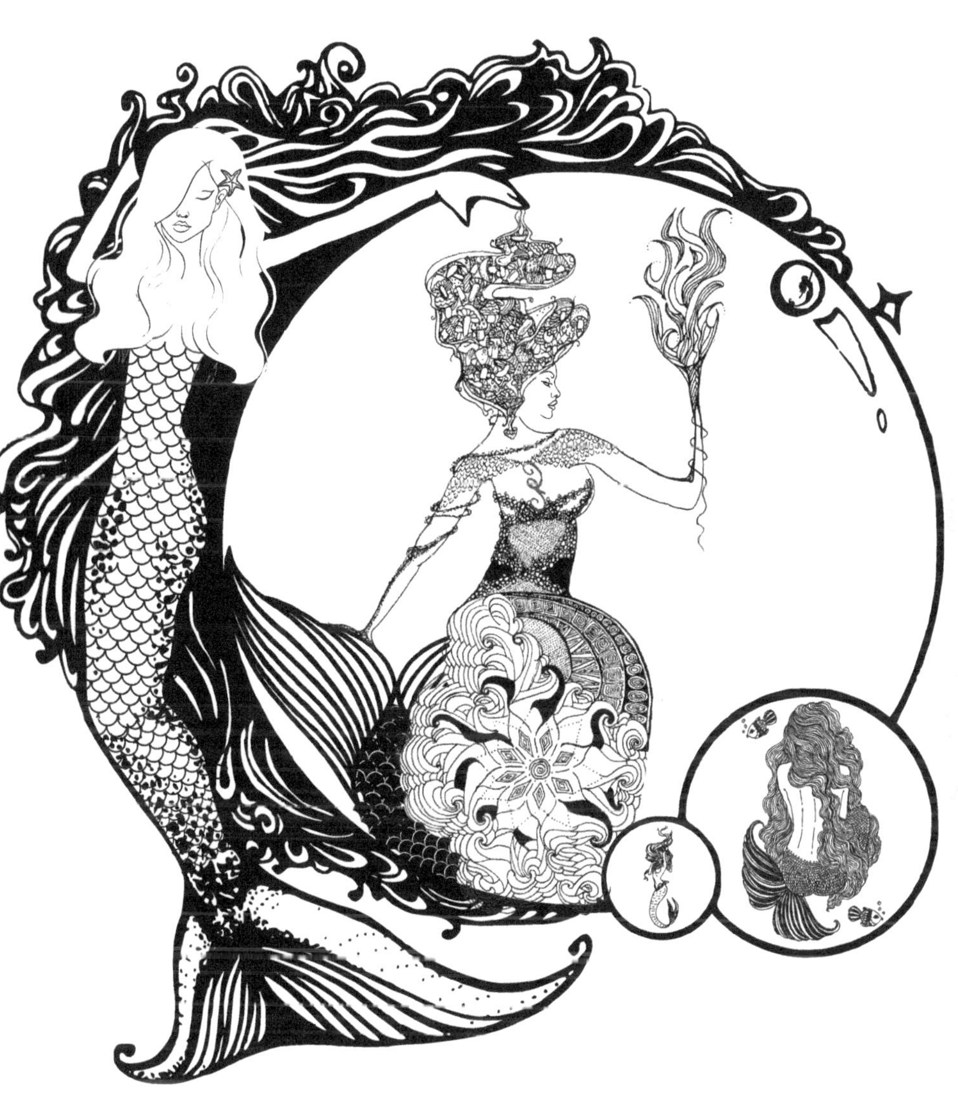

999

APPROACH

As the heart sings,
the mind hears a magical melody.
The soul hums an enchanting rhythm
and the body dances in harmony.
Allow your heart to love even if its been broken;
as one of these days your heart will play its final beat.
Nourish your body with health and healing;
as one of these moments the spirit will soar.
Let go of your worries, fears, and guilt;
as one of these breaths will set you free.
Be grateful for each magical moment;
as one of these seconds the clock will stop
and time will be meaningless.
Be here, now.
Celebrate the present,
it is a present.

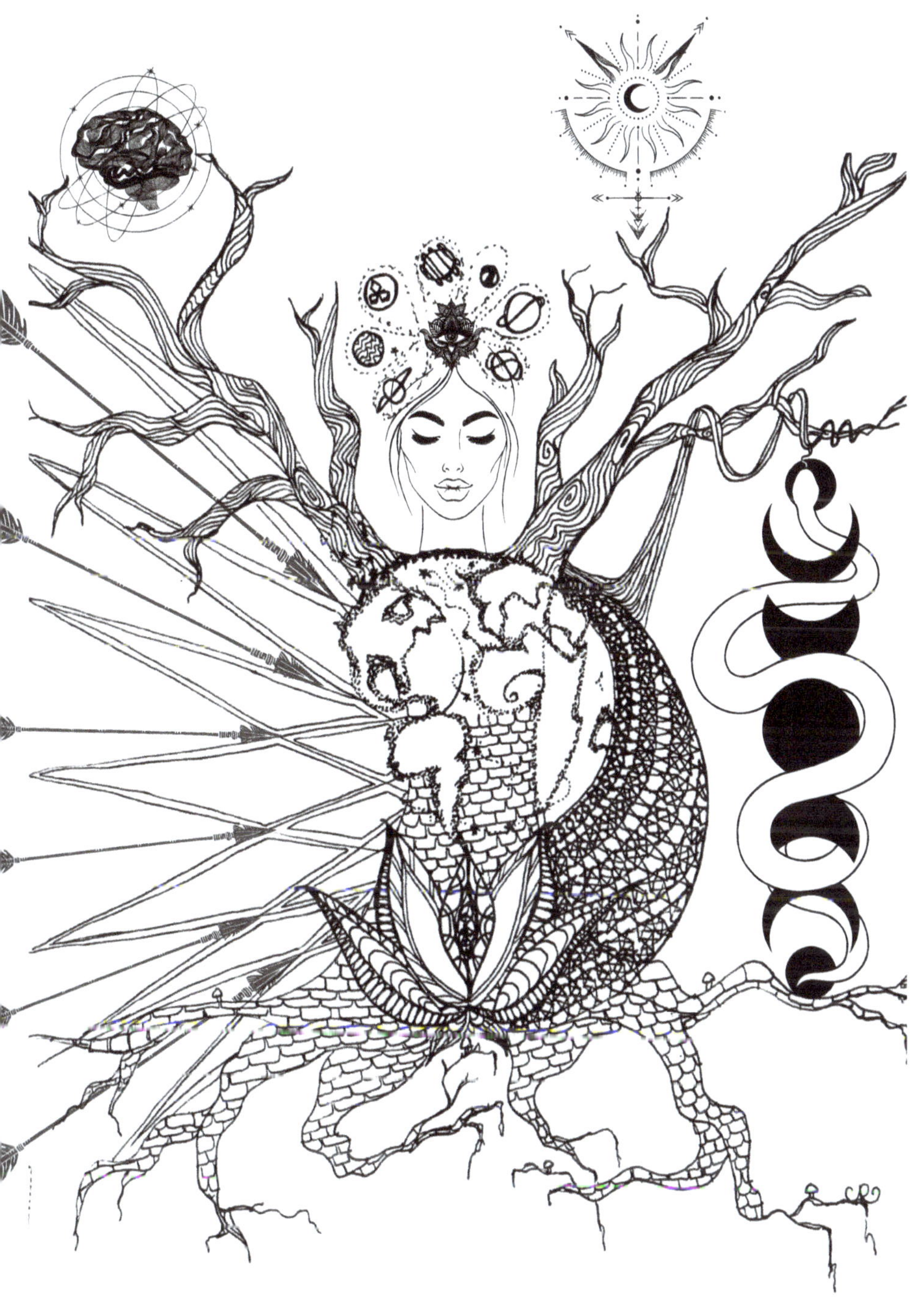

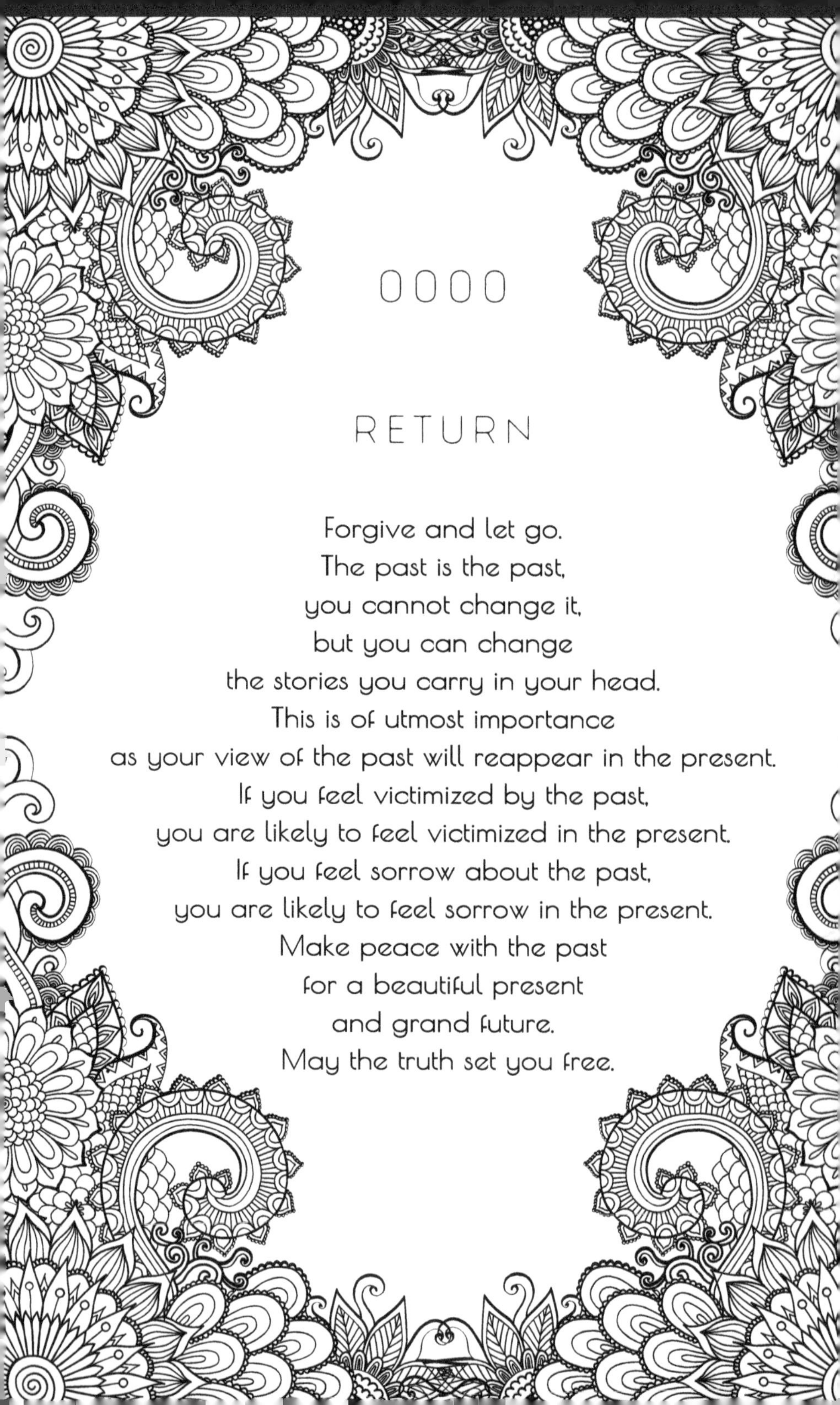

OOOO

RETURN

Forgive and let go.
The past is the past,
you cannot change it,
but you can change
the stories you carry in your head.
This is of utmost importance
as your view of the past will reappear in the present.
If you feel victimized by the past,
you are likely to feel victimized in the present.
If you feel sorrow about the past,
you are likely to feel sorrow in the present.
Make peace with the past
for a beautiful present
and grand future.
May the truth set you free.

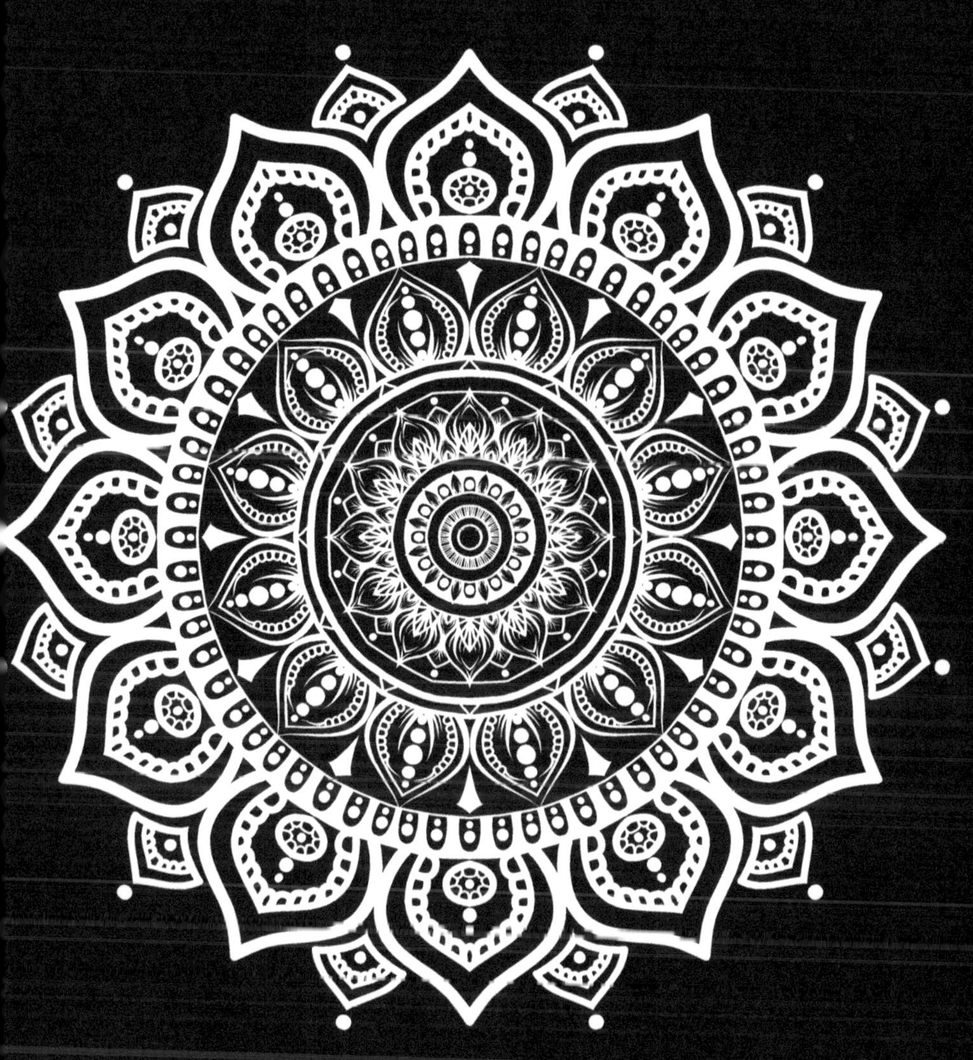

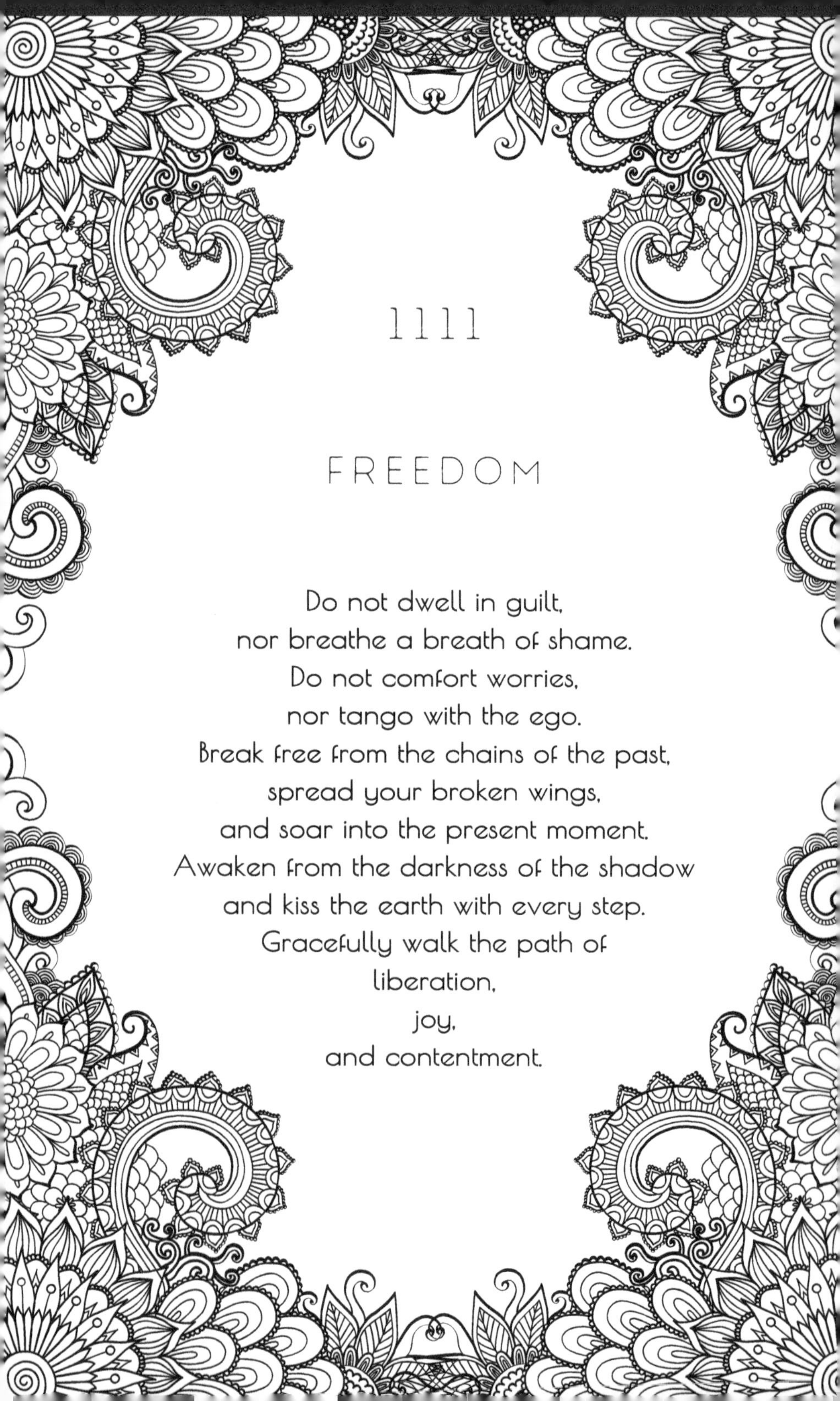

1111

FREEDOM

Do not dwell in guilt,
nor breathe a breath of shame.
Do not comfort worries,
nor tango with the ego.
Break free from the chains of the past,
spread your broken wings,
and soar into the present moment.
Awaken from the darkness of the shadow
and kiss the earth with every step.
Gracefully walk the path of
liberation,
joy,
and contentment.

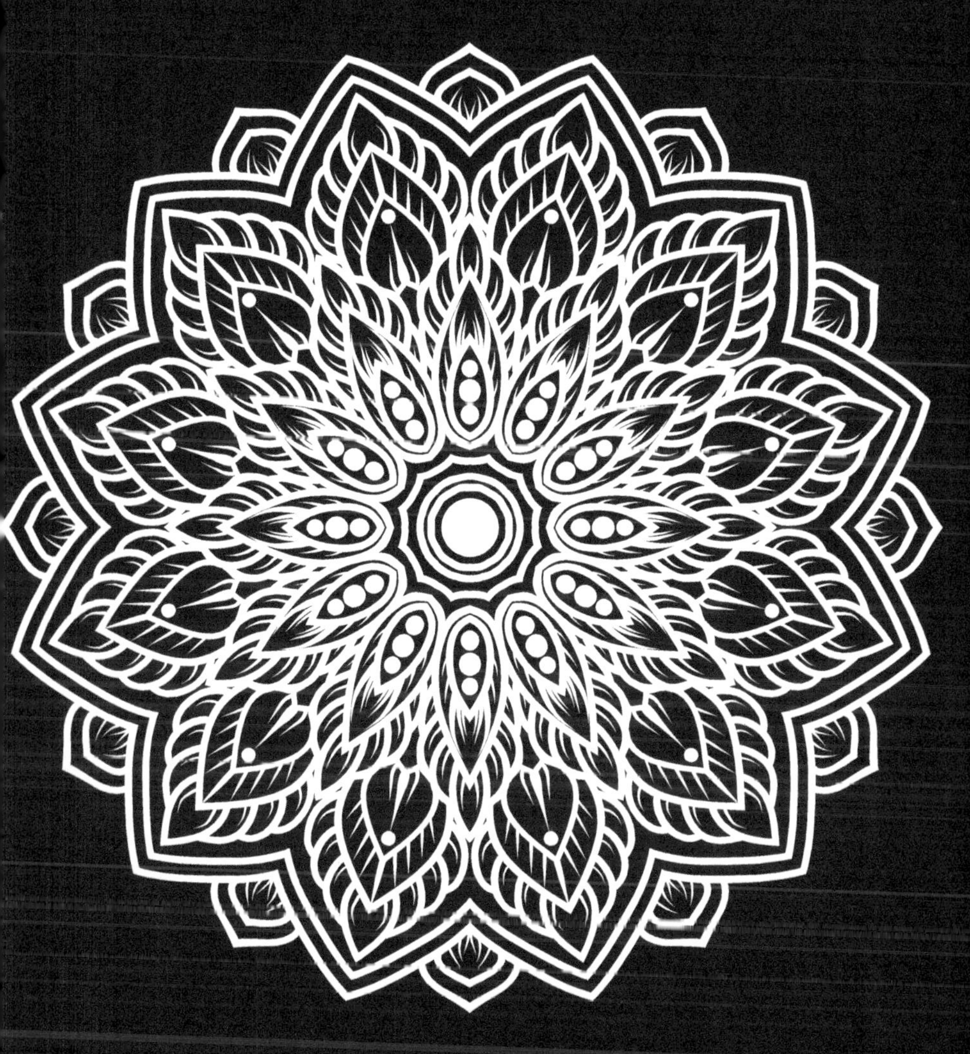

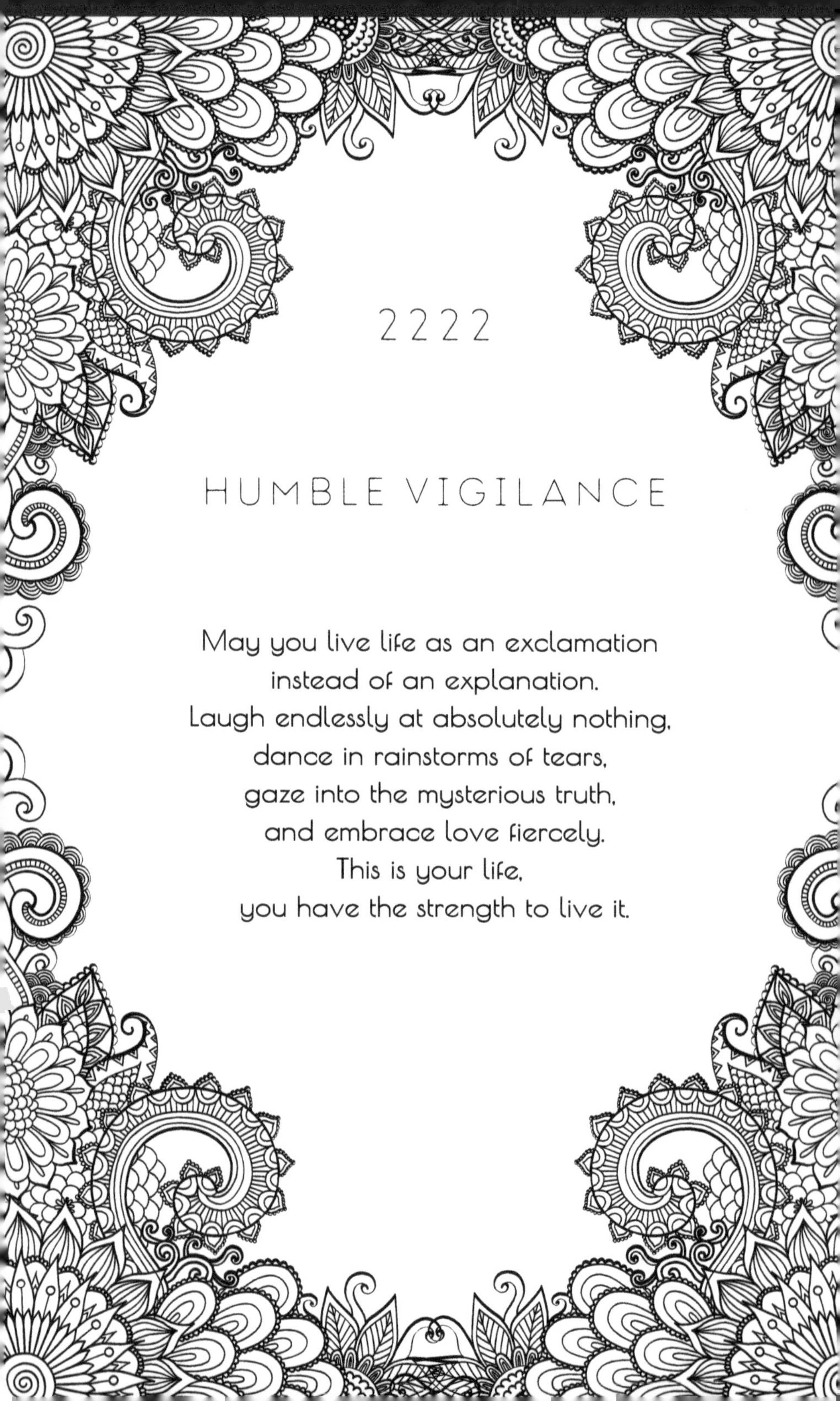

2222

HUMBLE VIGILANCE

May you live life as an exclamation
instead of an explanation.
Laugh endlessly at absolutely nothing,
dance in rainstorms of tears,
gaze into the mysterious truth,
and embrace love fiercely.
This is your life,
you have the strength to live it.

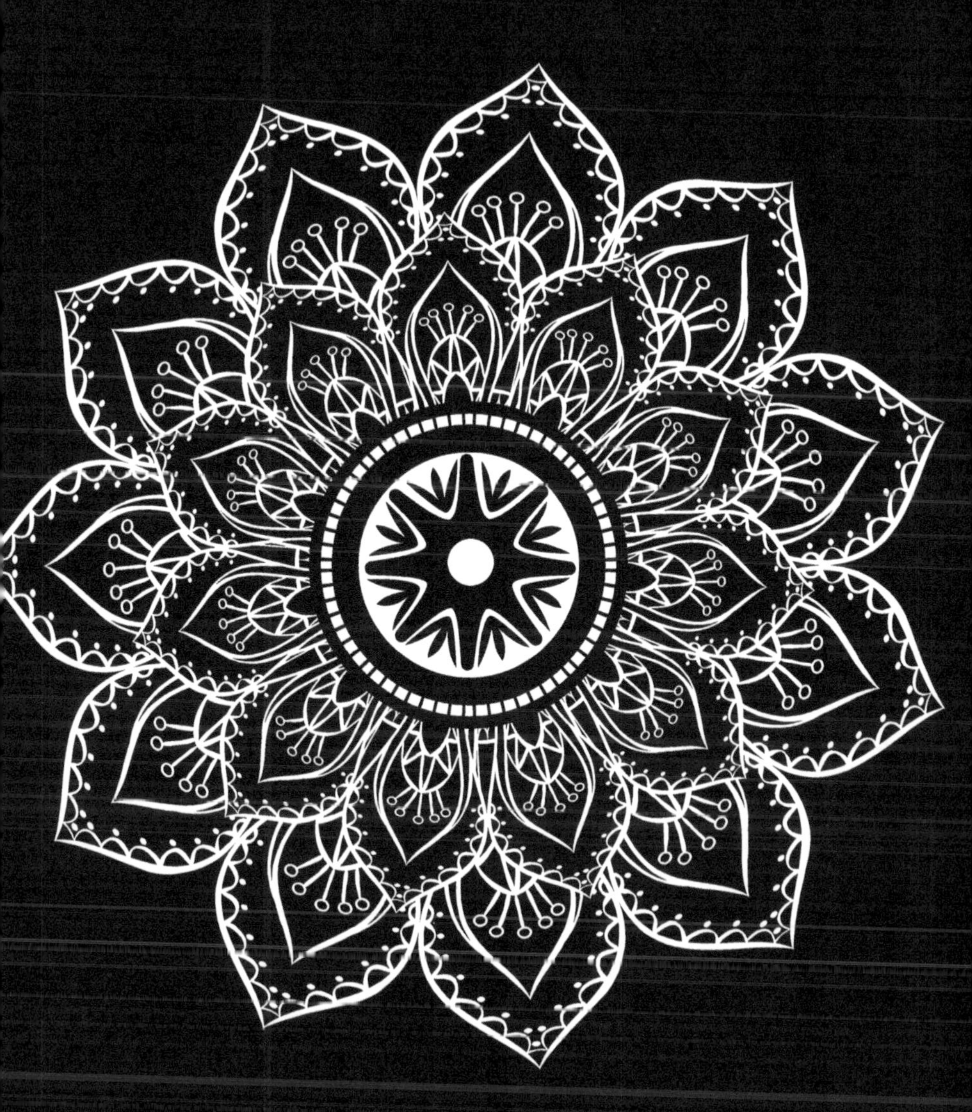

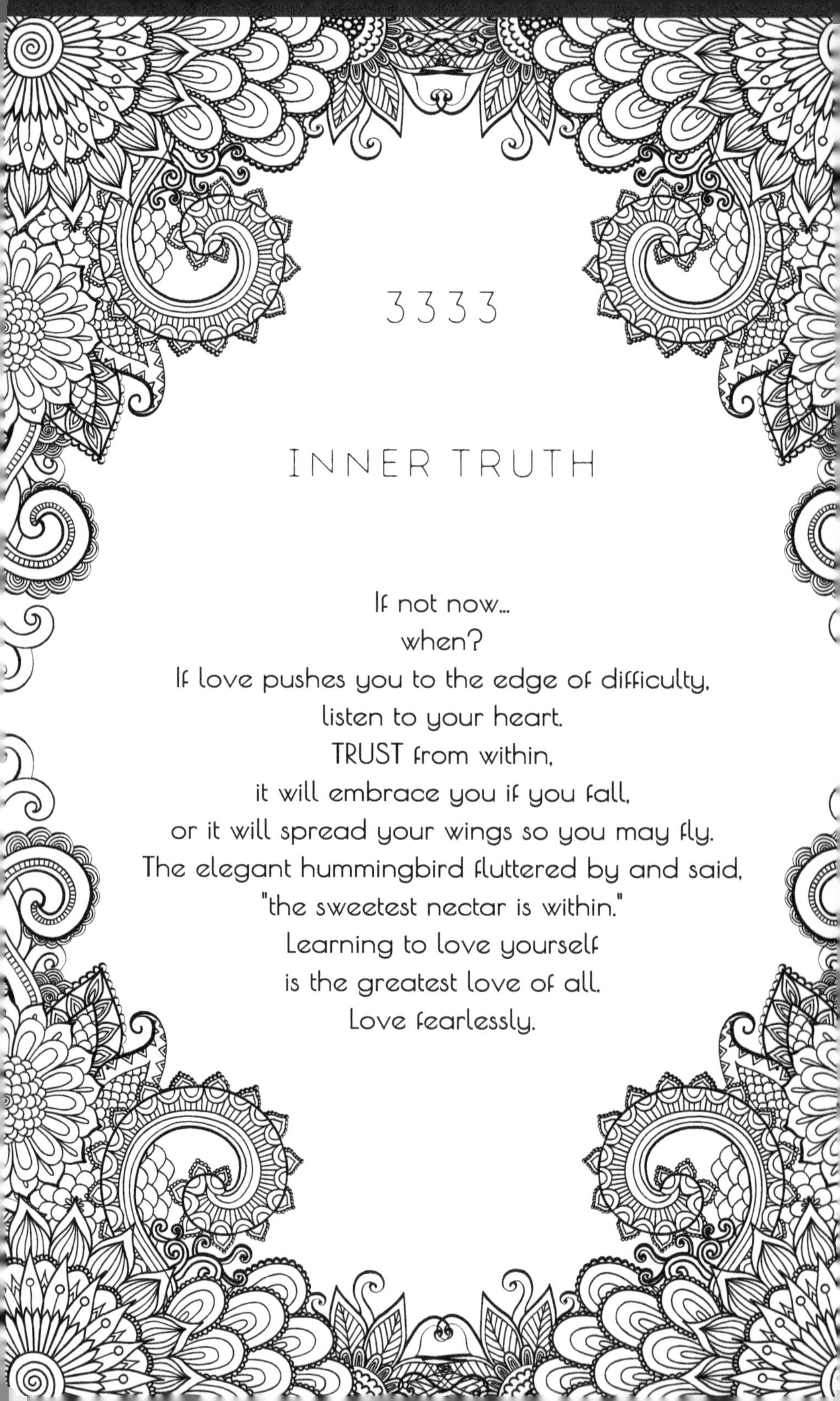
3 3 3 3

INNER TRUTH

If not now...
when?
If love pushes you to the edge of difficulty,
listen to your heart.
TRUST from within,
it will embrace you if you fall,
or it will spread your wings so you may fly.
The elegant hummingbird fluttered by and said,
"the sweetest nectar is within."
Learning to love yourself
is the greatest love of all.
Love fearlessly.

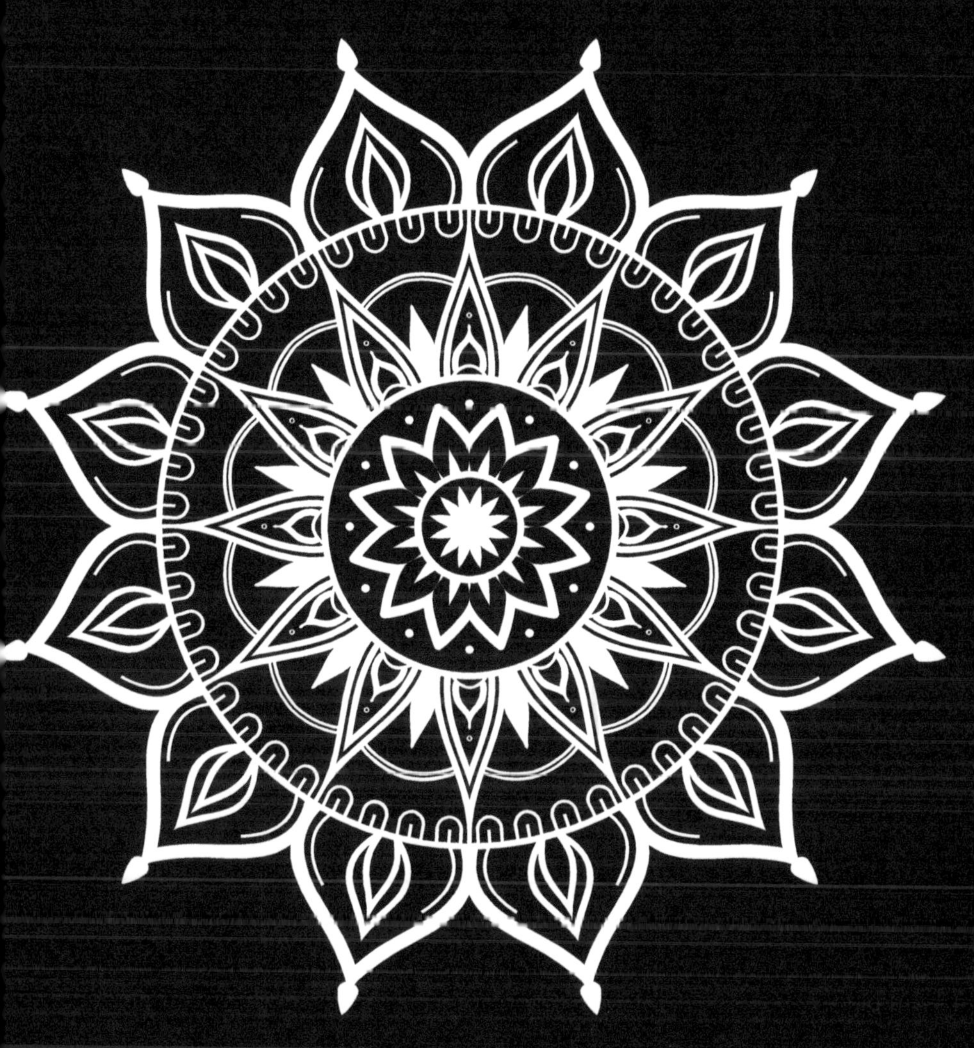

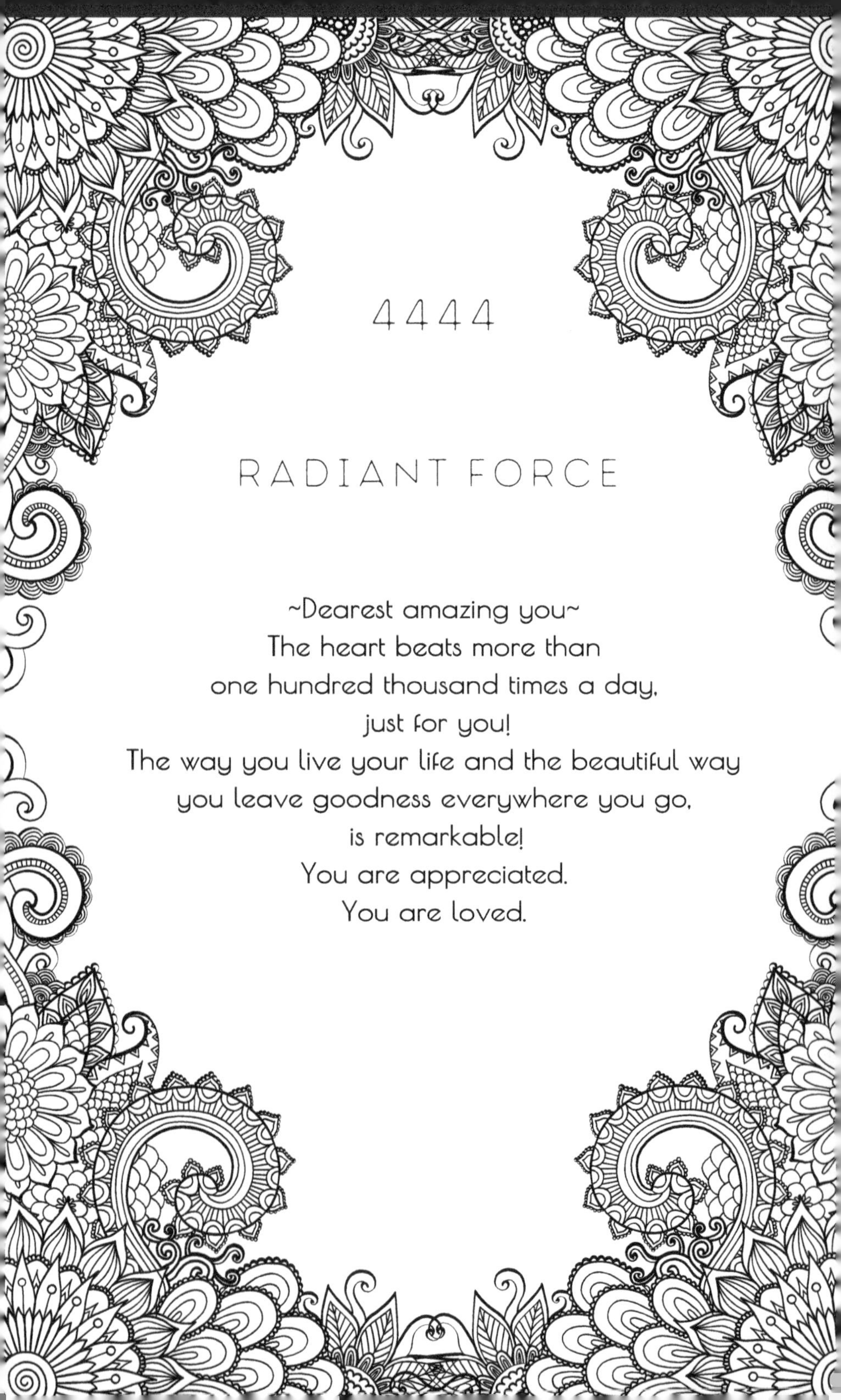

4 4 4 4

RADIANT FORCE

~Dearest amazing you~
The heart beats more than
one hundred thousand times a day,
just for you!
The way you live your life and the beautiful way
you leave goodness everywhere you go,
is remarkable!
You are appreciated.
You are loved.

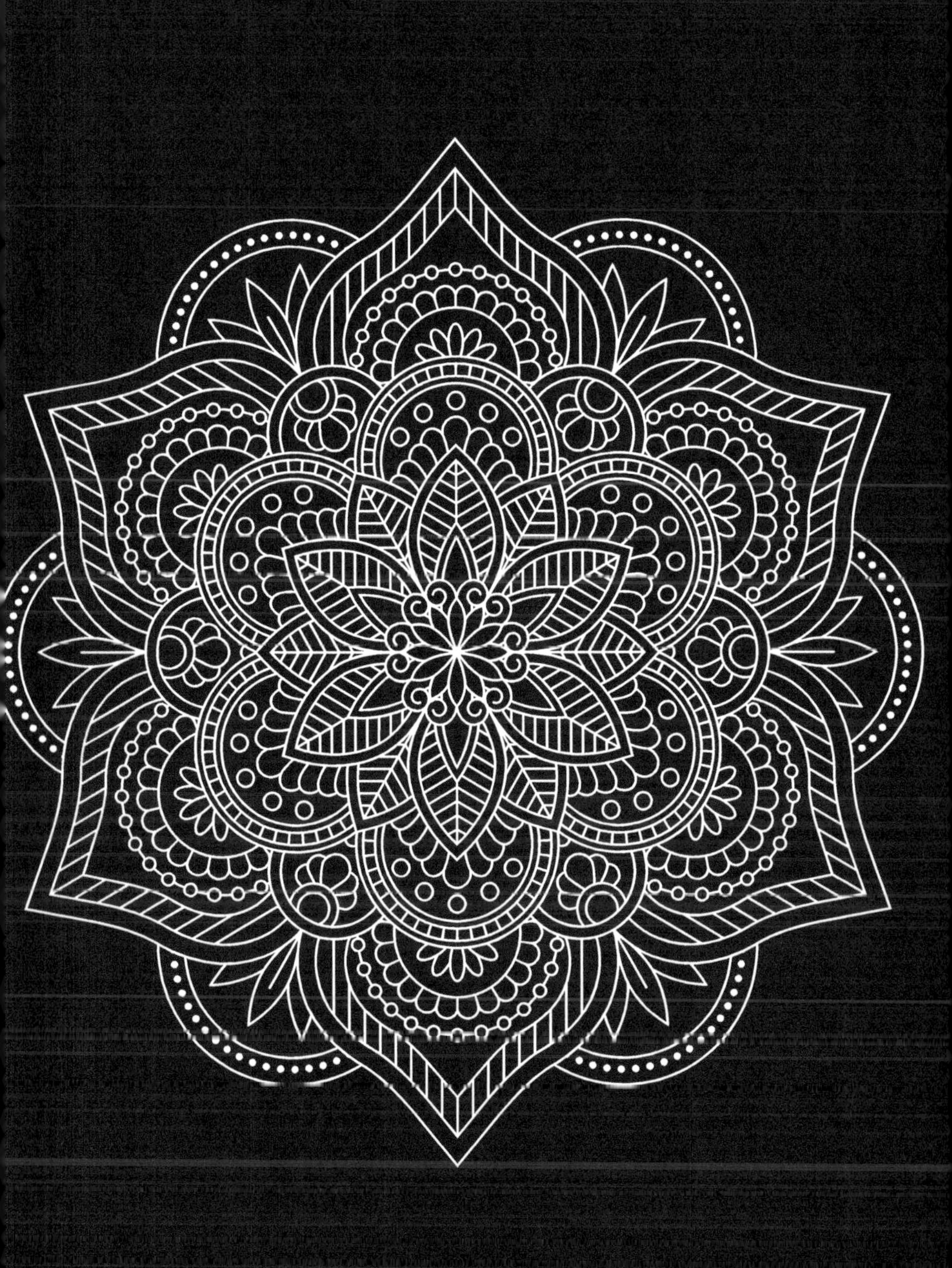

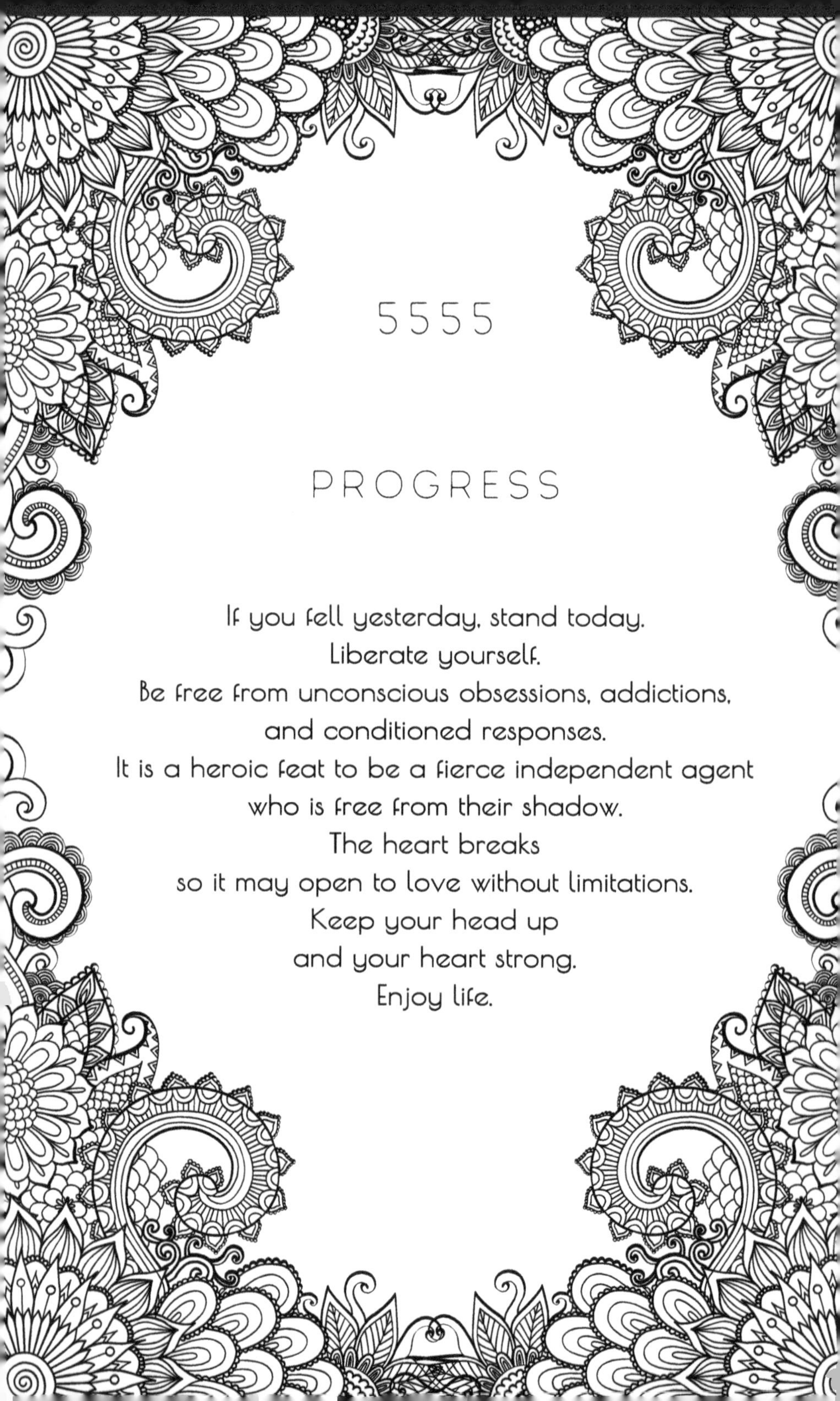

5555

PROGRESS

If you fell yesterday, stand today.
Liberate yourself.
Be free from unconscious obsessions, addictions,
and conditioned responses.
It is a heroic feat to be a fierce independent agent
who is free from their shadow.
The heart breaks
so it may open to love without limitations.
Keep your head up
and your heart strong.
Enjoy life.

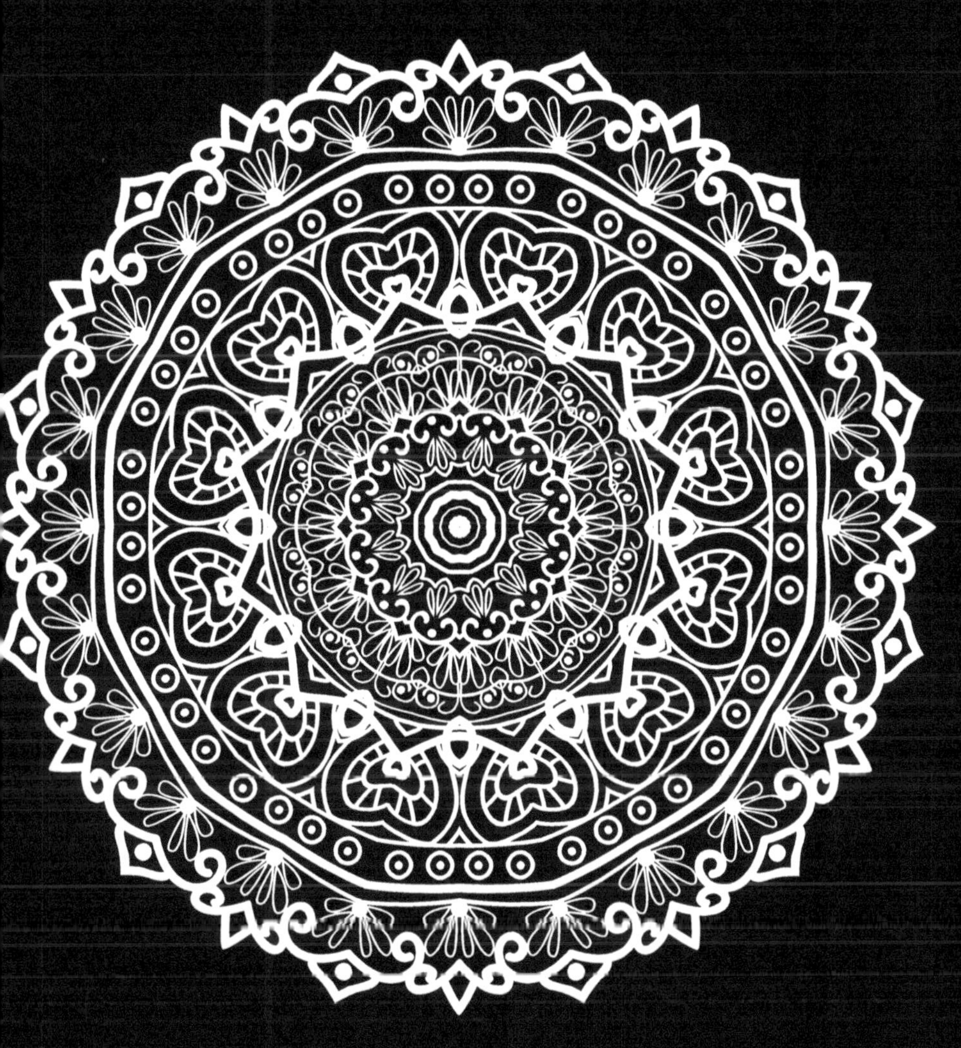

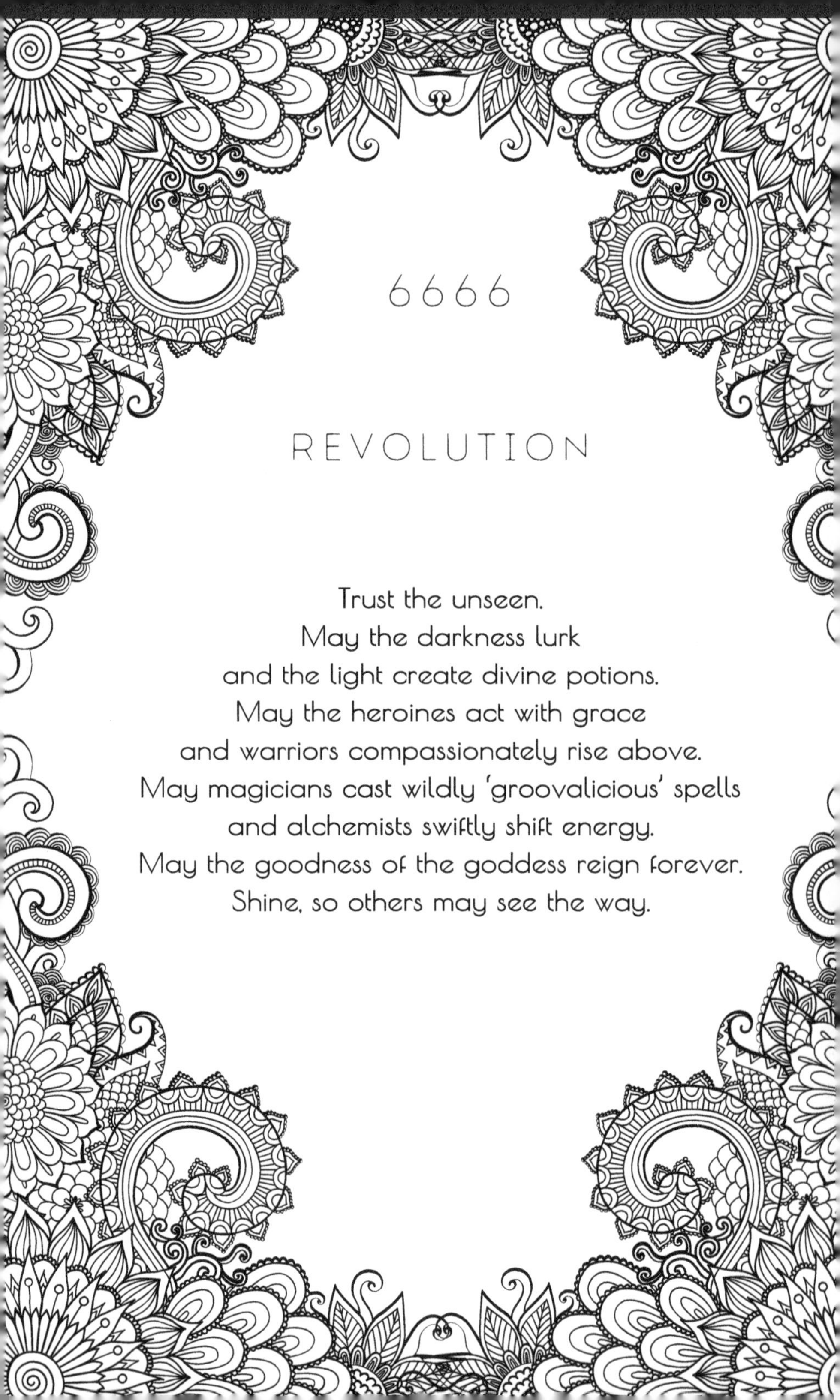

6666

REVOLUTION

Trust the unseen.
May the darkness lurk
and the light create divine potions.
May the heroines act with grace
and warriors compassionately rise above.
May magicians cast wildly 'groovalicious' spells
and alchemists swiftly shift energy.
May the goodness of the goddess reign forever.
Shine, so others may see the way.

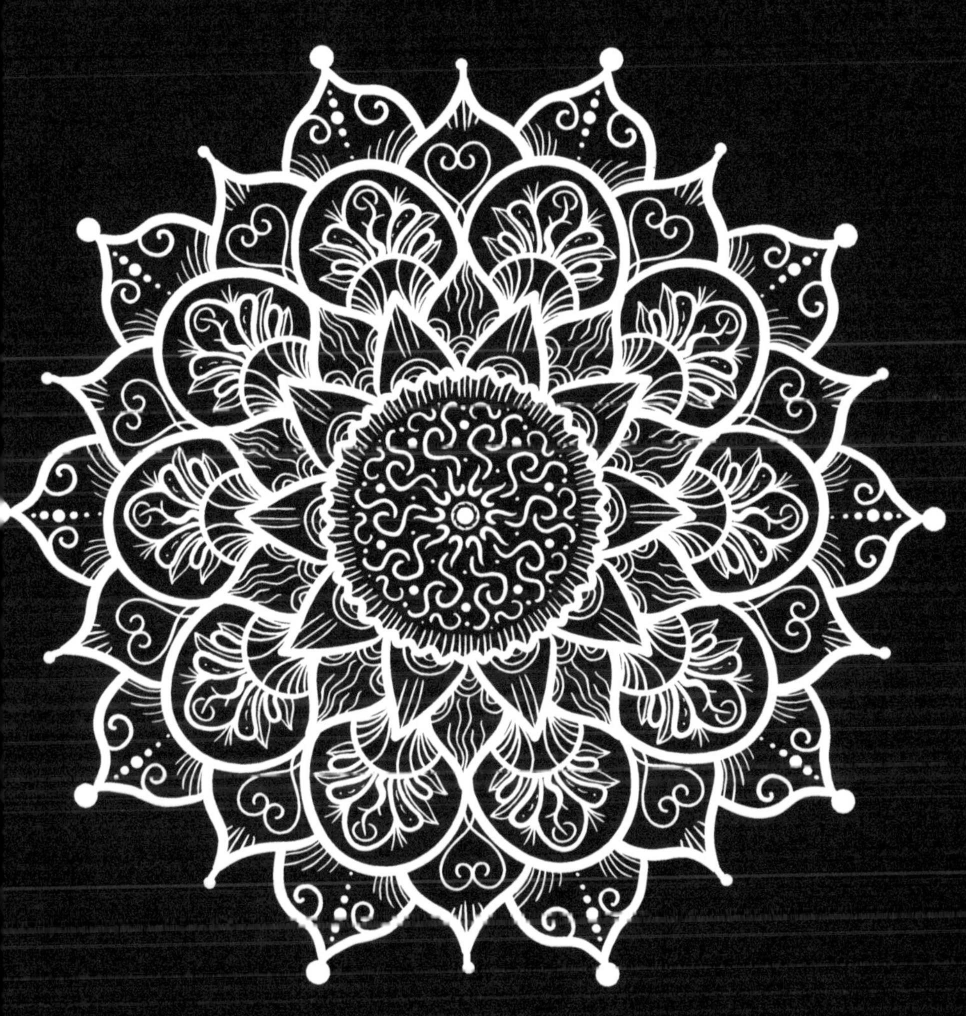

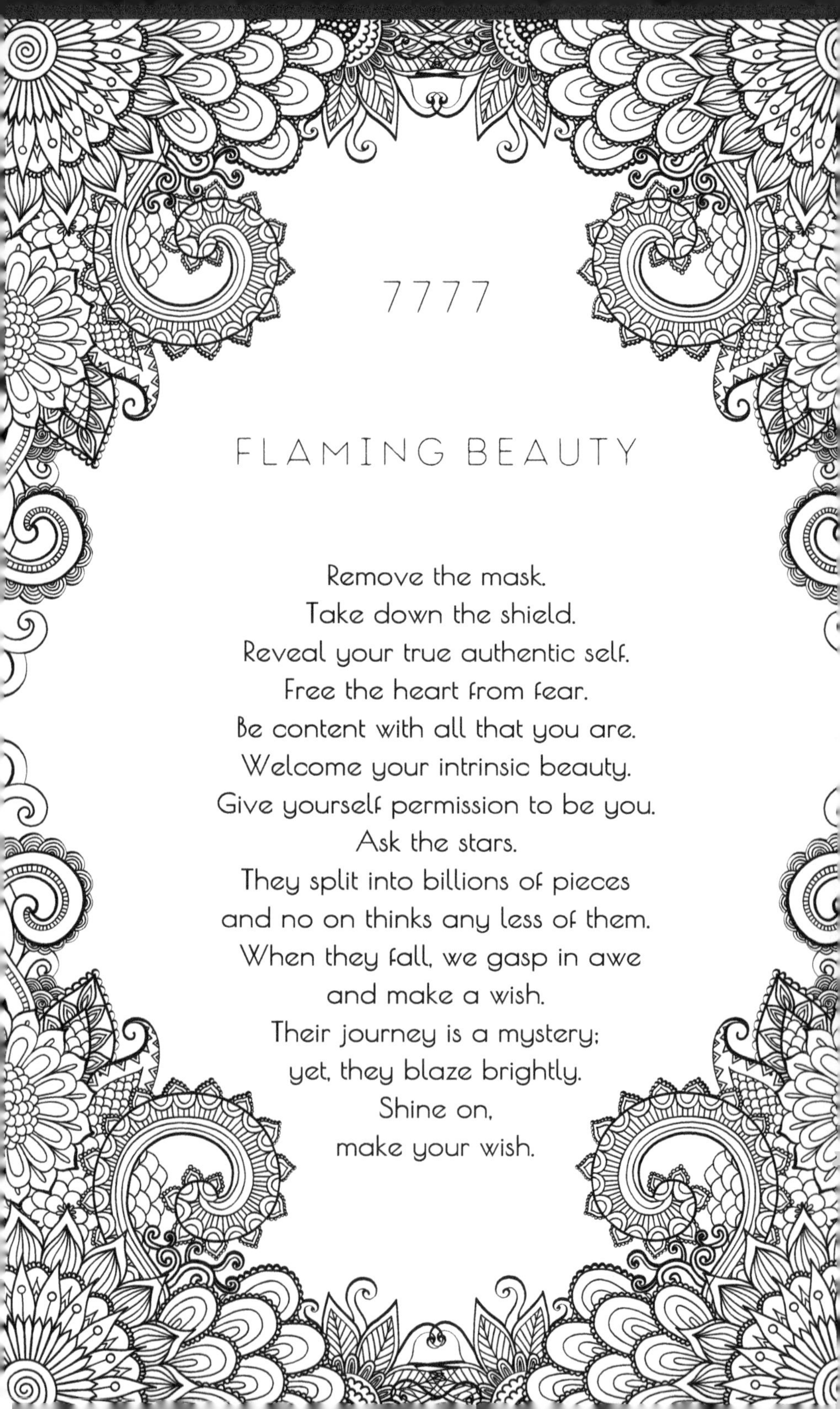

7777

FLAMING BEAUTY

Remove the mask.
Take down the shield.
Reveal your true authentic self.
Free the heart from fear.
Be content with all that you are.
Welcome your intrinsic beauty.
Give yourself permission to be you.
Ask the stars.
They split into billions of pieces
and no on thinks any less of them.
When they fall, we gasp in awe
and make a wish.
Their journey is a mystery;
yet, they blaze brightly.
Shine on,
make your wish.

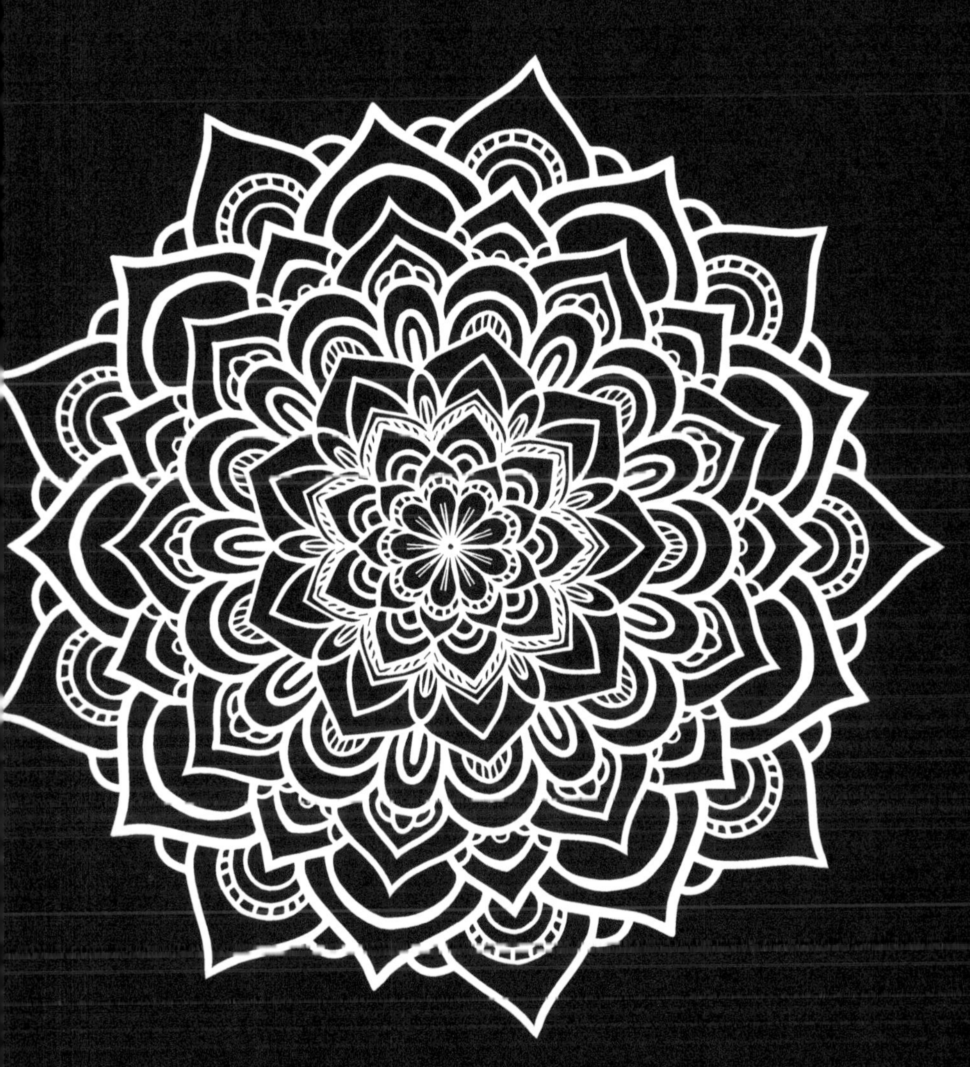

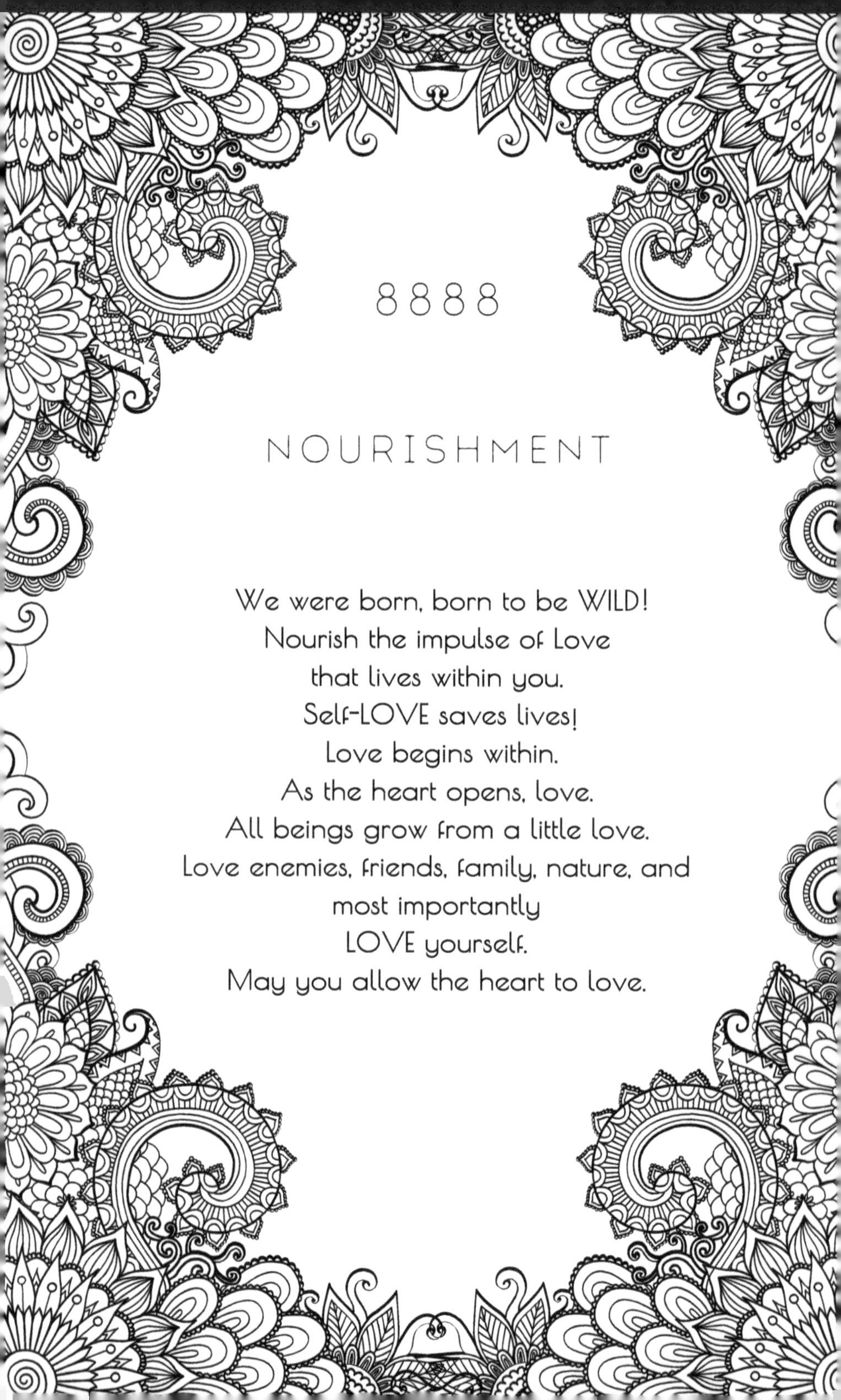

8888

NOURISHMENT

We were born, born to be WILD!
Nourish the impulse of Love
that lives within you.
Self-LOVE saves lives!
Love begins within.
As the heart opens, love.
All beings grow from a little love.
Love enemies, friends, family, nature, and
most importantly
LOVE yourself.
May you allow the heart to love.

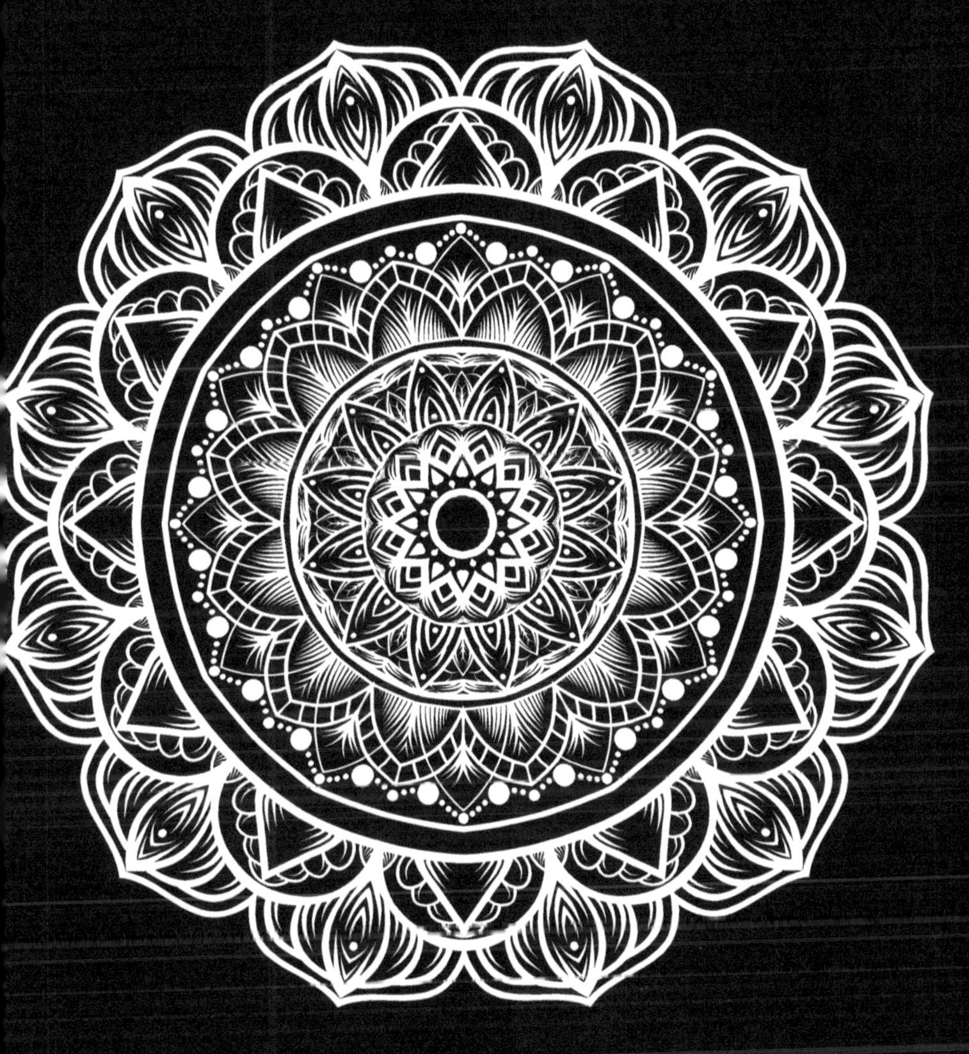

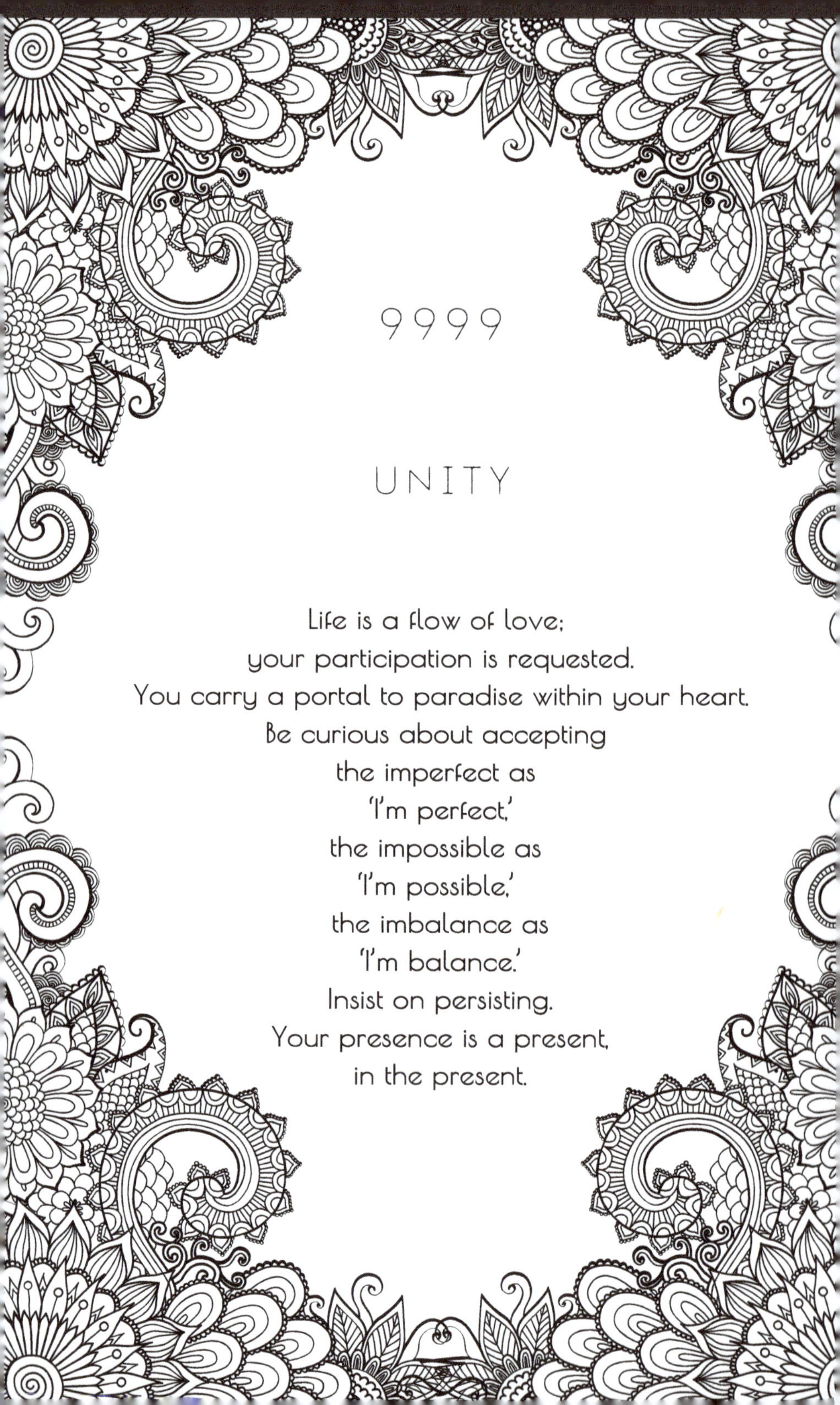

9999

UNITY

Life is a flow of love;
your participation is requested.
You carry a portal to paradise within your heart.
Be curious about accepting
the imperfect as
'I'm perfect,'
the impossible as
'I'm possible,'
the imbalance as
'I'm balance.'
Insist on persisting.
Your presence is a present,
in the present.

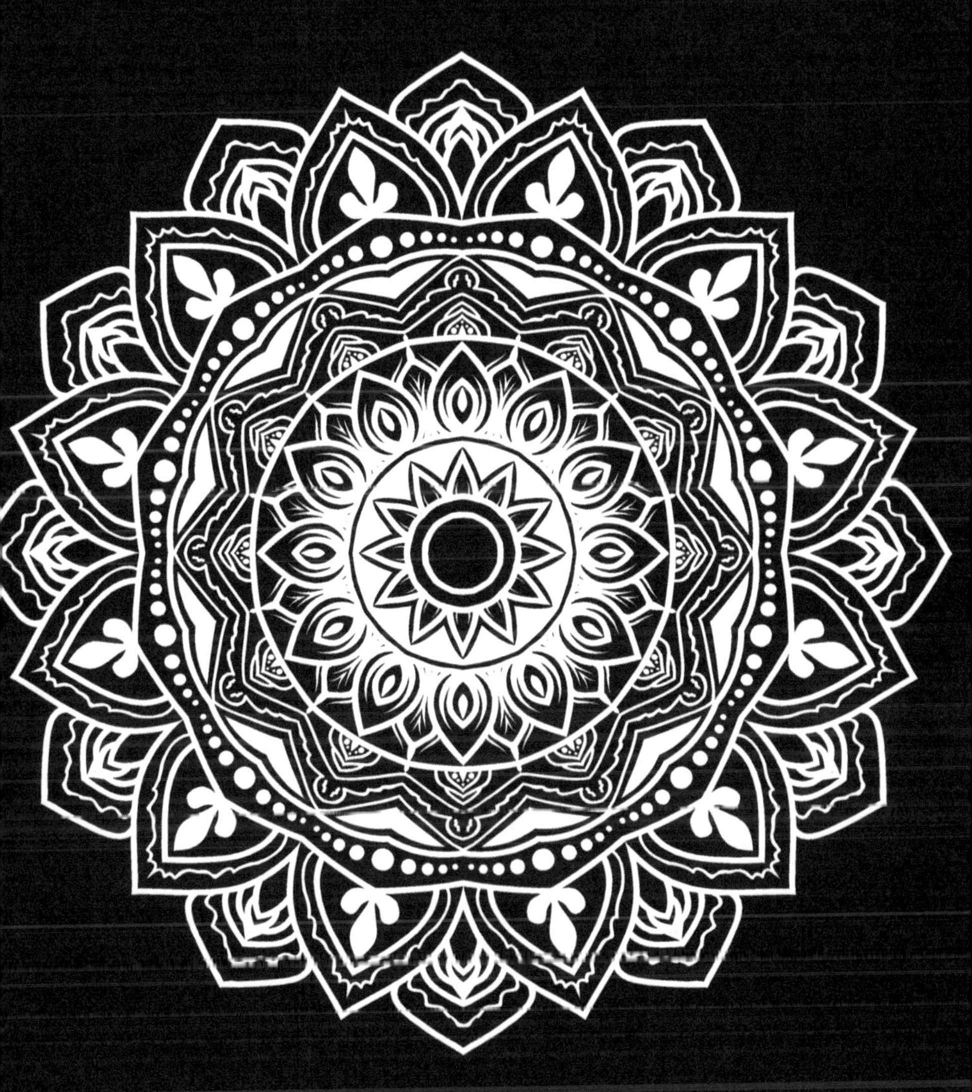

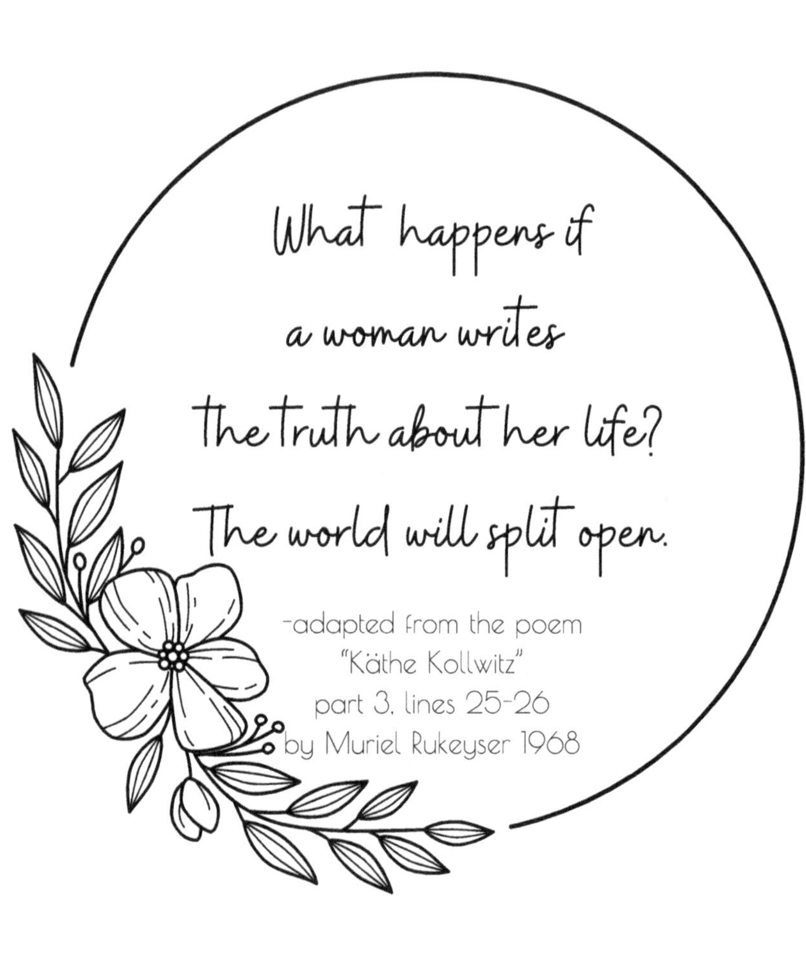
What happens if
a woman writes
the truth about her life?
The world will split open.
-adapted from the poem
"Käthe Kollwitz"
part 3, lines 25-26
by Muriel Rukeyser 1968

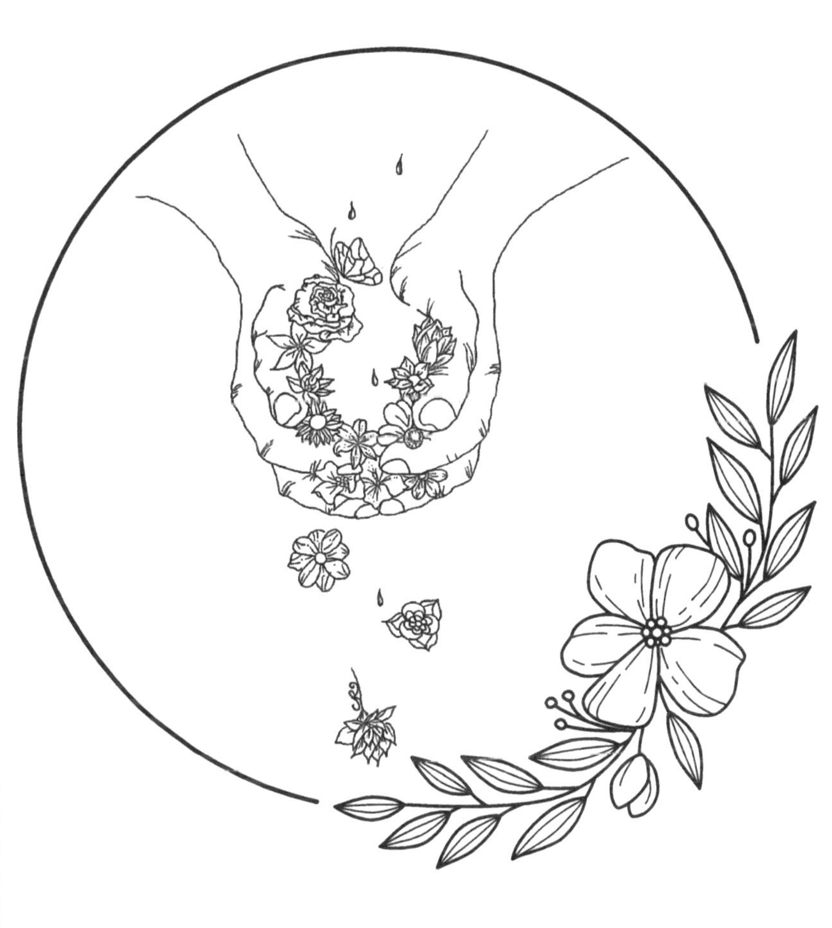